ROOTE

RECONNECTING WITH THE HISTORY OF THE CHURCH

EDWARD RHODES

ROOTED

RECONNECTING WITH THE HISTORY OF THE CHURCH

EDWARD RHODES

10 Publishing
a division of 10 of those.com

First published in Great Britain in 2017

British Library Cataloguing in Publication Data
A record for this book is available from the British Library

ISBN: 978-1-911272-62-5

Designed and typeset by Pete Barnsley (CreativeHoot.com)

Printed in Denmark by Nørhaven, Viborg

10Publishing, a division of 10ofthose.com
Unit C, Tomlinson Road, Leyland, PR25 2DY, England

Email: info@10ofthose.com
Website: www.10ofthose.com

CONTENTS

INTRODUCTION

This is a book about belonging. There's something about being human that makes us long to be part of something bigger than ourselves. We form societies and join clubs. Many people spend years researching their family tree, trying to find where they come from.

My contention is that becoming a Christian, becoming part of the church of Jesus Christ, is more like being part of a family than joining a club. So when we become Christians, we don't only gain new friends, or even new brothers and sisters; we also gain new ancestors! These ancestors shaped the Christian faith, which is why a strong faith in the 21st century needs at least some grounding in the 2,000 and more years of history which came before it. The church isn't a passing trend. Being thoroughly rooted in the past helps us, I believe, to stand stronger in the present, to know who we are and what we are about, even in the midst of great change.

As a younger Christian, I found myself strangely disconnected from this history. Naturally, I read my Bible. I also listened to sermons, many of which made reference to historical events. I loved watching documentaries and reading books about history. One year in my early twenties I even took part in a street drama about the life of the 18th-century evangelist George Whitefield, as part of the Brighton Festival. But even then there was something odd: almost all I knew about church history dated from the 16th-century Reformation onwards. It was also patchy, focusing on English-speaking evangelicals. As for the rest, I knew next to nothing. What little I had heard (such as the Crusades and the Spanish Inquisition) didn't sound good. It was as though the church had somehow disappeared from view as soon as the New Testament had been completed, only to re-emerge again when Martin Luther (supposedly) nailed his 95 theses to the door of the church in Wittenburg in 1517. Everything in between was a blur.

One day, it dawned on me that my understanding of the history of the church – that it had somehow all gone 'pear-shaped' at the end of the first century, only for the true faith to be restored during the Reformation in the 16th century – wasn't unlike the teaching of groups such as the Jehovah's Witnesses and Mormons, whose views I rejected. Yes, we had very different ideas as to how and when the faith was restored but we all seemed to agree that it had somehow been lost. I realised then that I needed to know more.

Since these doubting days of youth, I have become more and more convinced that this unawareness of the history of Christianity is a wider problem, particularly for evangelicals. Having raised these concerns to my church, I was asked to become involved in addressing them. I ended up teaching an intensive introductory course in church history to interns, and then wondering whether my work could be useful for a wider audience. This small book comes out of that wondering.

It is my hope that this book will help you to learn a little more about the story of the Christian faith between the end of the New Testament and the more recent past. Given the vastness of the subject, and my desire to keep the book both short and reasonably straightforward, this can only be an introduction, if that. Perhaps it makes more sense to think of it as a taster – trying to coax the reader into wanting more. If it does that, this brief book will have done all that I hoped that it would. It may challenge a lot of what we think we know. The terrain may also be a little bleak or difficult to walk through at times. Nevertheless, I still believe that the journey is worthwhile: knowing what happened in previous centuries makes it easier for us to make sense of the part of the story that we find ourselves in now.

A FEW EXPLANATIONS

In light of what I've said about the vastness of the subject, it makes sense to explain why I have included certain things but not others. I have tried to focus on important and well-known events, as well as those which relate to recent (and ongoing) controversies. I have also tried to keep the chapters more or less in chronological order. While Christianity spread far even while the

New Testament was being written, I have begun with a focus on the Eastern Mediterranean where it all started. I have then moved on to the lands where it flourished, particularly noting some key events in my own country, the United Kingdom.

This is a book written for Christians by a Christian. There are places therefore where the book may assume that the reader is a Christian believer. This is not to say that the book is of no use or interest to anyone who isn't a Christian – I hope that it is – but I thought it best to clear up any potential for misunderstanding at the outset.

If you think that too much of the story is dominated by male voices, then I agree with you. A good number of the leaders, thinkers and theologians of the church over the centuries have been men. I don't wish to deny or downplay the important role of women in the history of Christianity, only to note that their contribution has largely been less public, and that less of it has survived in the written sources. This isn't an excuse, of course, but it is important to note.

As a rule, Bible verses are taken from the New International Version (NIV) 2011. All dates are AD (or, if you prefer, CE).

APPLICATIONS

I have included suggested applications, or at least points to ponder, in Christian life and ministry, at the end of each chapter as well as questions for further study. This is a perilous task: it is not easy to translate the thought of one age into another, so readers should beware. Nevertheless, I do believe there are lessons that we can learn from history and I have written this book with a view to it being practical as well as informative.

SOME WORDS OF THANKS

It remains for me to give a huge thank you to Tim Jones, for his initiative, advice and encouragement, without which this book wouldn't even have been thought of, let alone written. Thanks are also due to my reviewers for their feedback and in helping me to develop a more accessible writing style. I remain grateful to my family for their ongoing and unstinting support and care. Finally, and above all, I would like to give glory and honour and thanks to the triune God, Father, Son and Holy Spirit, into whose communion of unending love I have, through grace, been invited and called.

1

THE EARLY CHURCH

The Apostle John was instrumental in raising up a new generation of believers, who would lead the young church in the years to come. This would be essential when those who had known Christ in the flesh – who had heard his voice, seen him with their own eyes and touched him with their hands (1 John 1:1) – had all died. Indeed, the other apostles gave their lives as martyrs[1] because of their faith in Christ.

Yet while John's friends stood up for the Lord by dying, he continued to speak up for the Lord in life. The New Testament tells us that a rumour even went around among Jesus' disciples that John, the youngest disciple, would never die (John 21:20–24). John himself set the record straight and, sure enough, he eventually died, in the mid-90s AD, having lived into old age and shared the gospel with many.

THE APOSTOLIC FATHERS

The next generation of Christian writers, who came after the Apostle John, are known today as the Apostolic Fathers.

These disciples of Jesus' disciples also left us their own written testimony. It is useful to consider a few examples of their writings to help us understand what was going on in the church as it entered the second century. We see that the church was already facing many of the issues that still plague us today.

Clement of Rome

Clement of Rome's letter to the church in Corinth (known as 1 Clement)[2] was written in the early to mid-90s AD – about the same time that the New Testament was finished. It would seem that a group of young men in Corinth hadn't been paying attention to what the Apostle Paul had tried to tell their parents and grandparents about the dangers of factions; they had overthrown the leadership of the church and replaced them with a new set of leaders more suited to themselves.

Clement pleads with the rebels not to tear the church apart, reminding them of what Paul had written and using examples from the Old Testament Scriptures (as well as familiar pagan stories)[3] to show how rebellion and factionalism can threaten the community by sowing disorder and pride. The behaviour of the rebels wasn't only a sin but also a scandal: a bad witness to the wider community in which the Corinthian Christians lived. For Clement, the visible unity of the Church and respect for leadership were very important.

Ignatius of Antioch

Ignatius of Antioch was one of the first Christian martyrs of Syria. As Bishop of Antioch (the leader of the Apostle Paul's former home church), he was a man of some influence within the new Christian movement. Perhaps it was because of this prominence that he became one of its first martyrs when the authorities started to crack down. Almost all that we have of his story comes from seven letters that he wrote while on his last, long journey from Antioch to meet the lions in the Roman arena, probably sometime between AD 98 and 117.

Like Clement, Ignatius stresses the importance of unity, arguing that each church should unite around a single local leader, the bishop (though he does also speak about there being a council of elders). His second key concern is the spread of a teaching which argued that Christ didn't really have a physical body but merely seemed to do so.[4] Ignatius insists on the reality of God becoming a human being in Christ and warns us of the dangers of over-spiritualising our faith. Finally, in a moving letter to the believers in Rome, he deals with the issue of his own forthcoming martyrdom, asking the Roman Christians to 'spare him' by not trying to prevent his death. Perhaps he was worried for their safety, or concerned that people might think he had denied the Lord to save himself. Most likely, he was simply ready to die and be with Christ, even though this eagerness for martyrdom may sound shocking to us.

The *Didache*

One of the more important writings from this period, and one that we'll come back to in the next chapter when we look at worship, is a guide on how to run a local church, known as The *Didache* (or 'Teaching'). The writer of The *Didache* wants the church to be concerned about the risk that Christians could fall under the spell of charlatans, out to make money for themselves under the cloak of religion. The writer also warns against the opposite error, that of missing the leading of the Holy Spirit working through genuinely gifted prophets and teachers. The *Didache* is also important as the first Christian document to explicitly mention the controversial issues of abortion and the sexual abuse of children. So, even though it is an ancient text, many of its concerns remain deeply relevant today.

The Shepherd of Hermas

The longest of the writings of the Apostolic Fathers, and perhaps the most enigmatic, is *The Shepherd of Hermas*. This was a very popular book with early Christians – so popular in fact that, for a long while, it was a serious candidate for inclusion in the New Testament.

The *Shepherd* begins with a series of visions by the main protagonist, Hermas. In one of these visions, an 'angel of repentance' appears, in the form of a shepherd, and he goes on to give lengthy instruction to Hermas about the Christian life through a series of commandments[5] and parables.

The Shepherd of Hermas is controversial in that it seems to teach that forgiveness is only available once for a serious sin committed after baptism and even then only if repentance takes place within a limited time. This belief lingered on for some time in the church, and showed itself in the tendency for converts to delay baptism until late in life, so as to reduce the risk of committing a serious sin between baptism and death.

Starting to live a new life

One thing that unites all these books is a strong emphasis on the importance of sincere repentance and holiness. For the early church, becoming a Christian meant starting to live a totally new life, no longer focused on yourself but centred on serving God and others. Early Christians reached out to help the wider society: burying the dead too impoverished to have made provision for a funeral; rescuing children abandoned by their parents; and serving the poor and others at the margins of the society in which they lived.

Some of the Apostolic Fathers describe this call to a new life by using the image of two ways: the 'way of life' and the 'way of death'. Those who live for themselves, or who commit evil acts, walk on the way of death. Those who live to serve God and others, especially those in need, walk on the way of life.

Now, this may sound a bit like 'legalism' to those of us raised in traditions which emphasise the grace of God, but I don't think that we should be hard on the Apostolic

Fathers' understanding here. They don't deny that God is gracious or teach that we can somehow earn salvation, but rather remind us that God's grace teaches us to live a godly life (see Titus 2:11–12).

THE APOLOGISTS – STANDING UP FOR THE FAITH

Standing up for what you believe in has always been a challenging business: trying to explain yourself in a way that makes sense to others; countering their arguments without becoming either too aggressive or overly defensive; facing ridicule and misrepresentation. None of this is easy. It can cost us. For the second-century apologists, who came after the Apostolic Fathers, it could be very costly indeed.

This talk about 'apology' could be confusing because the word has changed its meaning over time. It doesn't mean that these individuals were sorry for being Christians. The word 'apology' comes from an ancient Greek word *apologia*, which means a 'reasoned defence'. 'Apologetics', therefore, is giving a reasonable defence of what you believe.

The boldness of Justin Martyr

Justin Martyr's approach to apologetics was courageous indeed. As his name suggests, his boldness ultimately cost him his life. Justin took the brave step of writing an open letter to the Roman emperor and other leading figures, known as the *First Apology*[6] *for the Christians* (although, as we have seen, the *First Defence* would be a better translation of the title). In this, he openly identifies himself as a Christian, and seeks to defend his fellow Christians against three false accusations made against them: firstly, that they were atheists; secondly, that they were engaged in immoral acts; and thirdly, that they were disloyal to the emperor. Justin addresses all these charges, pointing to the sincere faith, devotion and loyalty of the Christians, even in the face of mistreatment by the authorities.

Justin then goes on to argue positively for Christianity. He uses the now familiar argument that Christianity is the fulfilment of Jewish prophecies. He also finds arguments from other sources – even pagan myths and the writings of Greek philosophers such as Plato could be seen as pointing to Christ. For Justin, it is Christianity which is the true philosophy. The *First Apology* ends with one of the most detailed accounts that we have from the early church as to how the Christians conducted their worship, which we will look at in more detail in the next chapter.

IRENAEUS AND THE KNOW-ALLS

One of the greatest threats that faced the early Christian movement was the rise of various teachers who tried to assimilate Christianity into existing Greek ways of thinking. As the second century progressed, several of these movements came into being, claiming to possess special knowledge which would enable their hearers to understand the 'real' truth behind what the churches were saying. Because of this emphasis on knowledge (in Greek: *gnosis*), these groups later became known as Gnostics (that is, 'those in the know' or, less positively, the 'know-alls').

The situation soon grew so serious that it became necessary for Christians to refute Gnostic teachings. This task was taken up by the second of our apologists, Irenaeus of Lyons, in a book which he called *An Exposé and Overthrow of what is falsely called Knowledge*, but which is more commonly known today as *Against Heresies*.

These Gnostics varied from each other in details but they all had a fairly negative view of matter and the physical world. One group, called the Valentinians (after their leader, Valentinus), argued that the God of the Old Testament, who made the material universe, was not the same God as God the Father. Valentinus's alternative model is rather complicated but goes something like this. In the beginning was the divine fullness (that is, God the Father). Out of this divine fullness proceeded (in pairs) 30 spiritual entities, known as 'aeons'. The 12th of these aeons, a female aeon called Sophia, sought to pry into the essence of the Father, but, being unable to do so, fell into agony. As a result of her fall, the creator of the world (identified with the God of the Old Testament) came into being. This creator of the world was unable to comprehend anything above himself, and so believed himself to be God. Christ, the Holy Spirit and a second Christ-figure, called 'Saviour', are, according to this teaching, later 'aeons' come into the world to enlighten us and restore us to perfection.

Like the earlier teachers whom Ignatius had faced, the Gnostics tended to deny that Christ had actually become a human being, instead seeing him as a spiritual entity who merely appeared as human. These teachers argued that this is what the Bible really taught and they gathered enough followers to concern Irenaeus. The Valentinians' complex system may sound bizarre to us. Even today, however, doubts about the relationship between true spirituality and material things, and as to whether the God of the Old Testament is really the same God as the Father of the Lord Jesus Christ, still linger on.

Irenaeus wrote his book to expose these sorts of arguments, not allowing them to hide behind Christian-sounding language. He also wasn't afraid to use humour, even ridicule. At one point he substitutes the names of fruits and vegetables for the names of the aeons: those 'delirious melons of Valentinus'.[7] As the Gnostics used the Bible to defend their ideas, so Irenaeus uses the Bible against them, explaining why the Scriptures don't really teach what the Gnostics claimed. This gives an idea of the types of opposing views that the early church was up against.

Irenaeus, Marcion and the Bible

Another of Irenaeus's opponents, Marcion of Sinope, visited the Roman church sometime around 140 to share his new understanding of the gospel with them. It would seem that Marcion loved new ideas – so much so, in fact, that he totally rejected the Old Testament, agreeing with the Gnostics in regarding the Old Testament God as an inferior being. Having rejected all of the Old Testament, he then went on to reject most of the New Testament as well, seeing Paul as the only true apostle of Jesus. As far as Marcion was concerned, the New Testament only contained a reduced version of Luke's Gospel and Paul's letters.

Marcion is important because he challenged the church to clarify what should (and shouldn't) be included in the Bible. From various writings of the time it is clear that the Old Testament,[8] the four Gospels, the Acts of the Apostles and the letters of Paul were already generally accepted by Christians as divinely inspired Scripture. There was, however, still some doubt as to which of the other books in circulation should be included in the New Testament. Various lists survive which include most of the books that we recognise, but there were some ongoing doubts about the books from Hebrews onwards. Finally, in 367, Athanasius of Alexandria (whom we shall meet in chapter three) provided the church with the authoritative list of the 27 books of the New Testament which we have today.

It is worth noting that Marcion's list of New Testament books didn't include a number of alternative accounts of the life of Jesus, many of which are written from a Gnostic perspective and therefore known as the Gnostic gospels,[9] even though these would appear to be sympathetic to his own beliefs. It seems that many of these alternative accounts were not yet available or known by the time he was writing. By leaving them out, Marcion therefore acts as a witness (albeit a 'hostile witness') against them, highlighting that they were written later than the authentic testimony of the original apostles.

SUGGESTED APPLICATIONS

This overview of the early church is very informative and (perhaps) interesting, but what possible application can it have to Christians now?

Well, for a start, the early church has things to teach us about persecution. In the West at least, persecution is not (for now) as strong a threat as it sometimes was when the Apostolic Fathers were alive, and Western Christians should be wary about screaming 'persecution!' when things don't go our way. Nevertheless, Jesus did warn us that we would face trouble in this world (John 16:33), so we should be prepared to encounter opposition.

The early Christians, for example, didn't involve themselves in activities such as eating out in pagan temples, which excluded them socially. Worse than that, their refusal to take part in the cult of the emperor was, to many of their neighbours, a sort of treason. It is worth thinking about what the modern-day equivalent of these challenges might be. Even if we don't literally lose our lives for Christ, all Christians are called to a type of martyrdom in dying to their old life of sin ('the way of death') to live for Christ instead.

The importance of unity is another obvious application, and one that we'll come back to in a later chapter when we talk about the need to understand one another better. Here the challenge is the importance of showing respect to leaders. In the West, our culture warns us to be wary of authority (sometimes, it is sad to say, with good reason), which is why 1 Clement and the letters of Ignatius are so countercultural. This is not to say that anyone should be undiscerning or tolerant of evil. As the *Didache* shows us, it is undoubtedly right to oppose corrupt and spiritually abusive leadership, but we should also be wary of the risk of running to the opposite extreme.

We can learn from the apologists the importance of being able to give an answer for the hope which we have (1 Peter 3:15). As Christians, Jesus calls us to love the Lord with all our minds as well as with all our hearts and souls (Matthew 22:37). We can't just disengage our brains, especially when others are looking to us to give answers. Of course, we can't know everything, and claiming to have answers when we don't is silly, but it is right for us to engage with our faith intellectually, as well as with our emotions and actions. It is, however, worth questioning whether Irenaeus of Lyons's approach of seeking to support his arguments by ridiculing his opponents is necessarily the most fruitful one.

QUESTIONS FOR FURTHER STUDY

1 How well do you handle opposition to your beliefs?

2 Have you thought about living for Christ as being a sort of martyrdom before? How would this work in your life?

3 What is your attitude to authority figures? How should we respond to abusive leadership? Or to rebellion?

4 How well prepared are you to defend what you believe? How could you become better prepared?

2

WORSHIP

Worshipping God has always been at the very heart of what it means to be a believer. The church is first and foremost a worshipping community. If then we want to understand the early church, it makes sense for us to pause for a while and take a look at their worship.

Worship can be a controversial topic. Different styles and approaches exist across Christianity from formal and ceremonial at one end to charismatic and seeker-sensitive at the other. Differences of opinion on this subject can divide denominations, even generations, from one another. Sadly, churches have been torn apart by worship wars, fighting about how best to serve God on a Sunday morning.

HOUSE CHURCHES

In the New Testament local churches are often described as meeting in people's homes. The letters of Paul, for example, make mention of a church meeting in the house of Priscilla and Aquilla (Romans 16:3–5; 1 Corinthians 16:19) and the Christians in Jerusalem are described by the book of Acts as meeting not only in the temple but also from house to house (Acts 2:46). Furthermore, there is archaeological evidence of houses being converted into church buildings, as with the mid-third-century house church in Dura Europos. These house churches seem to have been somewhat larger than the house groups or similar meetings which are familiar to many Christians today. (The Dura Europos house church had room for around 50 people.) They provided a way for believers with larger homes to contribute to the community of faith.

The house churches of the early Christian period were largely a response to the fact that Christianity was effectively illegal in the Roman world prior to 313, and sometimes faced persecution. This often prevented local church communities owning their own buildings or meeting openly. Similar household-based meetings are a feature today in parts of the world where Christians need to worship in secret, away from the prying eyes of hostile authorities. This situation inevitably made the modern 'seeker-sensitive' approach impossible: it simply wouldn't have been safe to bring outsiders into the community unless there was good reason to think that they were already committed to the faith. Evangelism and mission therefore had to take place elsewhere.

THE SUNDAY SERVICE

This need for the church to meet secretly could feed rumours about what was really going on in their meetings. It would seem that there were stories circulating that accused Christians of things like cannibalism and sexual immorality. Perhaps this is why Justin Martyr ends his *First Apology* with such a lengthy account of what really went on at a Sunday worship service. He wanted to dispel the rumours.

Justin begins his account by reminding us that Christians don't only meet on Sundays but are 'always together', and that the wealthier members often come to the aid of the poorer. Nevertheless, each week, on 'the day called Sunday' the believers come together for a regular time of worship, where the 'memoirs of the apostles or the writings of the prophets' are read out and then explained to the people by the 'Ruler'[10] in a sermon. The people then stand and offer prayers to God, as bread, wine and water are brought in, to be blessed by the Ruler and served to the congregation as the Lord's Supper. Portions of the Lord's Supper are taken by the deacons to those who cannot be present at the service. Worship ends with a collection of money, which is used to help the widows and orphans plus those who are sick, in captivity or who through 'any other cause' are in need.

What Justin seems to be describing here (and other writers confirm this)[11] is that the worship of the early church was fairly structured by the middle of the second century. This does not necessarily mean that early church services were repetitive and boring. A good example to illustrate this is a wedding. At such an occasion there are predictable moments when certain people stand up and say specific words such as vows, speeches and toasts. Even at a less traditional wedding, the ceremony is unlikely to be entirely spontaneous! Yet none of this ceremony means that the wedding isn't full of celebration, love and joy. So it should be with worship. The celebration of the Lord's Supper was originally part of a meal, which itself looks forward to a wedding feast yet to come (see Matthew 26:28–29; 1 Corinthians 11:25–26; Revelation 19:9).

THE SACRAMENTS

The worship of the early church centred around the sacraments (or 'mysteries' as they were often called) of baptism and the Lord's Supper. Different denominations within Christianity disagree both as to how many of these sacraments there are and what exactly they mean, but almost all believe in baptism and the Lord's Supper. I will therefore focus on these two ordinances exclusively.

Baptism

The *Didache* provides us with a helpful description of baptisms in the early church:

> *Now, concerning baptism, baptize as follows: after you have reviewed all these things, baptize in the name of the Father and of the Son and of the Holy Spirit in running water. But if you have no running water, then baptize in some other water; and if you are not able to baptize in cold water, then do so in warm. But if you have neither, then pour water on the head three times in the name of the Father and Son and Holy Spirit.*[12]

Justin Martyr also provides us with the following:

> *As many as are persuaded and believe that the things we teach and say are true, and undertake to live accordingly, are instructed to pray and ask God with fasting for the remission of their past sins, while we pray and fast with them. Then they are brought with us where there is water, and are born again in the same manner of rebirth by which we ourselves were born again, for they then receive washing in water in the name of God the Father and Master of all, and of our Saviour, Jesus Christ, and of the Holy Spirit.*[13]

I am sure that it hasn't escaped your notice that Justin here treats being baptised as equivalent to being born again! This is controversial for evangelicals. It is clear, however, from reading these early Christian writers, that they didn't believe that baptism was simply a symbol of something which had already taken place. Instead, they believed that through the waters of baptism God objectively did something to the person being baptised, washing away their sins and giving them a fresh start.

The Lord's Supper

The early church's understanding of the Lord's Supper is equally controversial. One of the earliest descriptions of what the Lord's Supper meant to them comes from Ignatius of Antioch, writing just before his death, around the beginning of the second century. He labels as 'false teachers' those who don't believe in the reality of Christ's physical body and who therefore don't take communion because they don't believe that 'the Eucharist[14] is the flesh of our saviour Jesus Christ, which suffered for our sins and which the Father by his goodness raised up'.[15]

Justin Martyr likewise emphasises the presence of Christ in the Supper, explaining that 'the food consecrated through the word of prayer that is from Him, from which our blood and flesh are nourished by transformation, is the flesh and blood of that Jesus who became incarnate'.[16] Justin doesn't go into details as to exactly how this can be, and he does also speak of the meal as a remembrance of Christ. Nevertheless, it is clear that he, and others in the early church, understood communion as more than a simple reminder of Christ's death. These early Christians believed that the Lord himself is somehow present in and at his own Supper. The sacraments were widely seen as God actively communicating his grace to the church through physical means, such as water, bread and wine.

It is important to remember, though, that much of this was argued against teachers who held that the material universe was evil, and therefore that God couldn't (or wouldn't) use it as a means of showing grace to people. These questions would go on to become key points of controversy at the time of the Reformation in the 16th century.

GIFTS OF THE SPIRIT

With regards to God's ongoing miraculous work in the churches, Irenaeus of Lyons says:

> *Wherefore, also, those who are in truth his disciples, receiving grace from Him, do in His name, perform [miracles], so as to promote the welfare of other men, according to the gift which each one has received from Him. For some do certainly and truly drive out devils, so that those who have thus been cleansed from evil spirits, frequently both believe [in Christ] and join themselves to the Church. Others have foreknowledge of things to come; they see visions, and utter prophetic expressions. Others still, heal the sick by laying their hands upon them, and they are made whole. Yea, moreover, as I have said, the dead even have been raised up and remained among us for many years.*[17]

It would seem that the miraculous work of the Holy Spirit didn't cease with the deaths of the apostles after all, as some have argued. Why, then, were these miraculous gifts not as prominent in the following centuries of the church as they were at the beginning?

One answer comes from the experience of a hyper-charismatic group from the third century known as the 'new prophecy' or Montanism, after their leader Montanus. These Montanists[18] taught a strict morality, rejecting the possibility of forgiveness for serious sins committed after baptism, and had a strong emphasis on new prophecies from the Holy Spirit. Yet a strong sense of unorthodoxy hangs around the Montanist movement. This made later generations of Christians wary about claims of prophecies and other such spiritual gifts (though the possibility that spiritual gifts could be misused was already known, as chapter 11 of the *Didache* tells us). It should be noted, however, that there are still plenty of accounts of healings and other miracles throughout the centuries.

The influence of the Montanists may also have been another reason why the church felt the need to decide which books were and weren't part of the New Testament, in case new ones (presumably written while in a prophetic ecstasy) should start being added. There is even a claim that Montanus believed himself to be an incarnation of the Holy Spirit (although this accusation was made by his opponents).

SUGGESTED APPLICATIONS

This chapter has touched on some controversial issues and, in places, what I have written could be a stumbling block for some readers. I hope that this isn't the case. I am simply seeking to present what these early writers themselves taught rather than making any theological arguments myself, although there are doubtless lessons to be drawn. Could we, for example, describe our Sunday worship as sharing the celebration and joyful fellowship of a wedding feast?

The early church understood baptism and the Lord's Supper not simply as symbols but also as active encounters with God. How then should we think about our own baptism? How should we approach the Lord's table at communion? Do we expect to meet Christ there?

Likewise, miracles and spiritual gifts continued in the church in the second century. Is this something which we should look for today? The experience of the Montanists should perhaps give us reasons to be wary as to how these spiritual realities are expressed. However, we can acknowledge the risk that spiritual gifts may be abused, or counterfeited, without abandoning belief in them altogether.

QUESTIONS FOR FURTHER STUDY

1 Does your experience of worship on a Sunday resemble the joyful celebration which you would hope to find at a wedding feast? If not, why not, and what could you do about it?

2 Do you expect to encounter Christ at the Lord's Supper?

3 Do you think that spiritual gifts, such as healing and prophetic utterance, are something which we should look for today? If not, why not? If so, what can be done to protect against people abusing the gifts?

3

GOD IN THREE PERSONS

The Trinity was something in which the early church believed strongly and which features prominently in many of their creeds and confessions of faith. I was surprised by this emphasis as a younger man; I assumed that there would be a heavier focus on salvation. Indeed, it was reading through the so-called Athanasian Creed[19] in my bedroom one day in my twenties that first caused me to wonder whether I even believed the same faith as the early Christians. Now I see that this emphasis on the Trinity is indeed, at least in part, about salvation.

In this chapter we are going to take a look at the controversies surrounding the Trinity that arose in the fourth century. To clarify, though, the doctrine of the Trinity wasn't invented in the fourth century; it was implicit in the Christian message from the very beginning. For example, in the early descriptions of baptism that we looked at in chapter two, we see that people were baptised into the *name* (singular) of the Father, Son and Holy Spirit, a clear reflection of Jesus' command in Matthew 28:19. The idea that God is three persons sharing a single name, or identity, has its origins in the New Testament itself.

Furthermore, Irenaeus of Lyons (whom we met in chapter one) also alludes to the Trinity in his *Against Heresies*. Discussing the creation of the world, he says:

> *It was not angels, therefore, who made us, nor who formed us, neither had angels power to make an image of God, nor any one else … for God did not stand in need of these [beings] in order to the accomplishing of what He had Himself determined with Himself beforehand should be done, as if He did not possess His own hands. For with him were* always present *the Word and Wisdom, the Son and the Spirit, by whom and in whom, freely and spontaneously, He made all things, to whom also He speaks, 'Let Us make man after Our image and likeness.'*[20]

The Son and the Holy Spirit are described as being always present with God. There never was a time when they weren't around. God made the universe through them; they are his 'hands'. When God speaks to them, he speaks with himself.

While none of these writers actually uses the word 'Trinity' – this was first used by the writer Tertullian in the third century, and comes from the Latin *trinitas*, meaning 'threeness' – the core idea is there. Nevertheless, a detailed understanding of the doctrine of the Trinity was mostly developed by several early church councils (known as Ecumenical Councils),[21] usually in response to opposing teachings. The most well-known of these early councils, and the one that we'll focus on here, is the First Council of Nicaea of 325. Firstly, though, it is useful to take a step back and look briefly at the context of this famous gathering.

CONSTANTINE THE GREAT

In 304, the Emperor Diocletian ordered all people living within the Roman Empire to sacrifice to him as a god, or else face the consequences. This wasn't a new situation: his predecessor Decius had done the same half a century earlier. Diocletian's order ushered in a two-year period of empire-wide persecution for the church, which would linger on and off for a further seven. It is unlikely, at the time, that anyone imagined that Christianity would subsequently take its first step on the road to becoming the official religion of the Roman Empire. Yet this is what happened under Emperor Constantine.

Constantine had a vision in which he saw a Christian symbol[22] in the sky and heard the words: 'Under this sign you will conquer.' In 312, therefore, in a fight with a rival at Milvan Bridge on the outskirts of Rome, Constantine's soldiers went to battle with the same Christian symbol painted on their shields. When Constantine won a decisive victory, this sealed his sympathy for the Christian faith. In the following year he issued the decree of Milan, which legalised Christianity and brought an end to the official persecution.

Constantine's interest in the faith soon gave Christianity a favoured status. Despite a brief return to paganism under Emperor Julian (known as Julian the Apostate), Christianity became the official religion of the Roman Empire in 381 under Emperor Theodosius I, and the old pagan religion was suppressed.

ARIUS AND ATHANASIUS

However, this new legal Christian church almost immediately faced a crisis. The unity of the church was threatened by Arius, a church elder, who denied that the Son of God was eternally divine. While Arius did believe that Christ was divine in some sense, he also taught that he was created, that he wasn't of the same essential being as God the Father and that there was a time before he existed. This last point became a sort of Arian slogan – 'There was when he wasn't'. Arius's teaching caught on in a big way.

Arius was opposed by a man named Athanasius, who was unbending in his rejection of Arius's teaching, standing firm against all opposition (of which there was a lot) to defend the eternal divinity of the Son of God. Athanasius's name is therefore remembered in the saying 'Athanasius against the world'. For his trouble, though, Athanasius endured banishment as well as facing a number of false accusations, including one that he had killed a man named Arsenius, cut off his hand and used it for magical purposes! Arsenius, you will doubtless be glad to hear, was later found alive and in possession of both his hands.

The importance of this theological dispute to Athanasius can be seen in his book *On the Incarnation*. He teaches, firstly, that human beings have become separated from God, the Source of life, and therefore have become subject to eternal death. Secondly, Athanasius writes that God himself, not wanting humanity to perish, has himself become a human being in Jesus Christ, in order to reunite us with God and thus with eternal life. For Athanasius, then, it was the incarnation – God becoming a human being – that enables us to be saved. If Christ wasn't eternally divine, as Arius taught, how could his incarnation reunite anyone with God?

THE FIRST COUNCIL OF NICAEA

In order to deal with the growing divisions within the church caused by this controversy, the Emperor Constantine called a council of bishops to give a judgement on the dispute. The idea of calling a council to resolve church disputes can trace its origins back to Acts 15 and the Council of Jerusalem.[23] Yet while Constantine summoned the council and presided over its meetings, he had no vote in its proceedings.

The council met in 325 in the city of Nicaea, in what is now Turkey. Around 200 or 300[24] bishops were present, a number of whom still bore the scars of earlier persecution – visible reminders of their refusal to bow to imperial pressure. The council considered several statements as to what the church's teaching should be. The first, proposed by Eusebius of Nicomedia (who later baptised Constantine) and worded along Arian lines, was soundly defeated. A second proposal, by Eusebius of Caesarea, seems to have followed a 'can't we all just get along?' approach, opting for a wording which avoided having to come down strongly on either side of the debate. Ultimately, the First Council of Nicaea decided in favour of the Athanasian position, drawing up their conclusions in the following statement (known as the Creed of Nicaea), which was to be read in churches during Sunday worship:

We believe in one God the Father almighty, maker of all things visible and invisible.

And in one Lord Jesus Christ, the Son of God, begotten of the Father, uniquely begotten, that is, of the being of the Father, God from God, Light from Light, true God from true God, begotten not made, of one being with the Father, through whom all things were made, things in heaven and things on the earth; who for us human beings and for our salvation came down and was made flesh and became a human being, suffered and rose on the third day, ascended into the heavens, and is coming to judge the living and the dead.

And in the Holy Spirit.

But those who say – 'There was when he was not' and, 'Before he was begotten, he was not' and that, 'He came into being from what is not' or those who allege that the

> *Son of God is 'of another substance or being' or 'created' or 'changeable' or 'alterable' – these the catholic and apostolic church declares accursed.*[25]

One key teaching of the Creed of Nicaea is the 'eternal generation' of the Son – the idea that the Son is eternally 'begotten' (that is, born or generated) by the Father from his own being. As C. S. Lewis once noted, beings tend to beget beings of the same sort as themselves.[26] God, therefore, begets God. And because God is eternal, the one whom God begets is also eternal. There never was a time when the begotten wasn't. The Son of God, who is 'of one being with the Father', is therefore divine in the same way that the Father is divine.

There were of course those who disagreed, although not as many as is sometimes supposed. Only 18 members of the council voted against the new creed. Of those, only two – Secundus of Ptolemais and Theonas of Marmarica (both from Arius's homeland of Libya) – still refused to agree, even when it meant losing their positions as bishops and going into exile.

CONTROVERSY CONTINUES

Arianism wasn't ended by the First Council of Nicaea – a dispute like this couldn't be resolved simply by a declaration. Arians won sympathy because they were often denied communion on the grounds that they were false teachers. Furthermore, the Emperor Constantine seems to have started having second thoughts. Indeed, Athanasius of Alexandria, who had so valiantly and unwaveringly defended the eternal divinity of Christ, spent most of his later life in exile.

Later councils were called at Constantinople (now Istanbul) in 381, at Ephesus in 431, at Chalcedon in 451, in Constantinople again in 553 and 680, and again at Nicaea in 787 to discuss ongoing controversies about the person of Christ.[27] The last of these seven councils (which dealt with whether the incarnation of Christ meant that images could be used in worship) is the most controversial among Protestants.[28]

Most of the teachings about Christ that the church rejected at these councils tended to deny either his full humanity (as though he were simply God walking around in a body suit, pretending to be human) or else his full divinity. The humanity of Christ – that he was God in the flesh; God become a human being – seems to have been the bigger stumbling block. Even among Christians today there can be a tendency to over-spiritualise Christ – to downplay the reality of his human life.

However, Gregory of Nazienzen, a fourth-century church leader from Cappadocia in Greece, made an important observation that followed on from Athanasius's teaching. Speaking about Christ, Gregory said, 'That which he has not assumed he has not healed, but that which is united to his Godhead is also saved.'[29] In other words, Gregory agreed with Athanasius that Christ saves us by uniting our humanity to God. If Christ hadn't taken on our full humanity, he couldn't have done this. Likewise, if Christ is not fully God, then union with him is not union with God, and therefore we are neither healed nor reunited to the Source of life from whom we have become estranged.

THE SPIRIT FIGHTERS

It wasn't only the divinity of Christ that people denied. During the later fourth century a group known to the church as the Spirit Fighters came into being. These denied the divinity of the Holy Spirit. In response to this challenge, the First Council of Constantinople proclaimed the following clause, defending the divinity of the Holy Spirit, which was then added to the creed: 'And [we believe] in one Holy Spirit, the Lord, the Giver of life, who proceeds from the Father,[30] who with the Father and the Son together is worshipped and glorified, who spoke through the prophets.'

Thus by the end of the fourth century, the church had explained and defended its teaching on the Trinity – one God eternally existing in three persons: the Father (as eternal source of the Trinity); the Son (eternally fathered by the Father as God from God); and the Spirit (eternally proceeding from the Father and worshipped as God together with the Father and the Son).

SUGGESTED APPLICATIONS

Perhaps you are still confused, finding the doctrine of the Trinity hard to grasp. As finite human beings, we can't really expect to understand the inner life of the infinite God. Some may question the point of all this infighting and see the Trinity – the belief that God is somehow both three and one – as a bizarre mathematical puzzle or a contradiction. Yet the Trinity is far from being irrelevant or unimportant. Indeed, I would go so far as to ask whether there is any other teaching which is *as* important. The doctrine of the Trinity teaches us who God is and what he is like. The Catholic philosopher Peter Kreeft can explain it far better than I can:

> *People often think the idea of the Trinity is irrelevant. But no one thinks the idea that God is love is irrelevant. Yet if God is not a Trinity, God is not love, for you need more than one person for unselfish love. If God were only one person he could only be selfish love. At best, he could be a lover of human persons, but not Love itself. And then he would be dependent on those human persons; without them he would not be unselfish love. Only the Trinity allows God to be unselfish love in his own essential, independent being. The Father loves the Son, not himself; the Son loves the Father, not himself; the Spirit is the love between the Father and the Son, a love so real that it is a third Person.*[31]

The other key teaching that arose from these early councils and which is critical to our understanding of who Christ is, and what he means to us, is the incarnation. Jesus is God in the flesh. In Jesus Christ, God came down to us and became a human being, in order that he might save us. By uniting our humanity to his divinity, by living as we should have lived, and by dying on a cross on our behalf, he paid our debt, so that, one day we may be with him and, even more shockingly, be like him.

If God is essentially unselfish love, if God loves us so much as to become one of us and suffer for our sakes, then what sort of people should we be? What sort of love for God and for other people should we have?

QUESTIONS FOR FURTHER STUDY

1 Before reading this chapter, how important did you think that the doctrine of the Trinity was? Has this chapter changed your mind?

2 Which (if either) of these do you find the more difficult to believe: the divinity of Christ or the humanity of Christ?

3 If God is essentially unselfish love, then what sort of love should we have for God and for other people? How does this work in your life?

4

INTO THE WILDERNESS

Taking time out to focus on Christ without distraction – in a community of like-minded people, with the same aim and goal – has been an important part of my life as a believer. Indeed, some of the most special times where I have sensed the presence of God have been on Christian retreats, especially at Ashburnham Place in East Sussex. This desire to retreat from the world and seek God, even if only for a while, was important in the history of the early church. It led to the development of monasticism.

Many figures in Scripture (including the Lord Jesus himself) spent a season away from everything to fast, pray and reflect, often before making important decisions, but they all returned to life in the world afterwards. From the third century onwards, however, people began increasingly to seek a permanent life in the wilderness, often fleeing from what they saw as the worldliness and decadence of the church (then largely experiencing a relative period of calm from persecution – though not one that would last). The most popular refuge seems to have been the deserts of Egypt.

ANTHONY AND EARLY MONASTICISM

The rise of monasticism itself is often associated with the figure of Anthony the Great (c. 250–356).[32] While he was neither the first person to retreat to the wilderness nor even the first monk, his prominence is largely due to a biography of him written by Athanasius. Anthony's call to leave it all behind took place when, while attending a church service one day, he heard the Scriptures being read aloud. As Athanasius describes:

> *Less than six months had passed since his parents' death when, as usual, he chanced to be on his way to church. As he was walking along, he collected his thoughts and reflected how the Apostles left everything and followed the Saviour; also how the people in Acts sold what they had and laid it at the feet of the Apostles for distribution among the needy; and what great hope is laid up in Heaven for such as these. With these thoughts in mind he entered the church. And it so happened that the Gospel was being read at that moment and he heard the passage in which the Lord says to the rich man: If you will be perfect, go sell all that you have, and give it to the poor; and come, follow me, and you shall have treasure in Heaven. As though God had put him in mind of the saints and as though the reading had been directed especially at him, Anthony immediately left the church and gave to the townspeople the property he had*

> *from his forebears ... He did not want to encumber himself or his sister in any way whatever. He sold all the rest, the chattels they had, and gave the tidy sum he received to the poor, keeping back only a little for his sister.*[33]

Anthony went to live in caves and tombs in the desert, leading a life of severe austerity, fasting and prayer – a kind of daily martyrdom. However, after a couple of decades, his fame for holy living and miracle-working had made him an object of devotion to others, many of whom flocked out into the desert to see him, or to seek some miracle or word of teaching. In this way Anthony found himself unintentionally at the head of a small community of like-minded followers.

Anthony's story highlights the problem faced by these early Egyptian monks (known to history as the Desert Fathers and Mothers).[34] Their zeal to seek Christ and lead holy lives in the wilderness, far away from the corruption and temptations of civilisation, made them attractive to others seeking a similar refuge from the world. Thus the monks (whose very name conjures up the ideal of being alone)[35] found themselves living in communities.

BEING ALONE TOGETHER

Pachomius the Great (292–348), a former soldier turned monk, was one of the first people to see the need for organising these communities through a set of rules. He organised his community with separate cells (where monks could live alone) but centred around a communal area (where monks could gather together for meals and common worship). While there continued to be a few hermits, this regulated and communal approach soon became the norm. It balanced the ideal of solitude and focus on Christ with the ideal of a community of believers who could encourage and support each other. Pachomius is also said to have invented a prayer rope tied into knots to help monks keep track of their prayers – a method still used by some Christians today.

THE RISE AND FALL OF THE MONASTERIES

Despite these significant beginnings, the heyday of monasticism was still to come. Following the fall of the Roman Empire in the West to barbarian invaders in the fifth century, it was the monasteries which acted as transmitters and guardians of ancient learning, with their libraries of manuscripts. Far from Christianity wanting to take people back to the so-called 'Dark Ages', it was largely Christians who took them out of it in the first place.[36]

Benedict of Nursia (480–553) is a particularly significant figure from this time. He set up a number of monastic communities in Italy, governed by a set of spiritual and administrative precepts known as the Rule of St Benedict. These helped to maintain and develop the monastic tradition within Christianity in the aftermath of the fall of Rome. Benedict's rule became the most commonly applied monastic system in the West in later centuries and can be summed up in the phrase *ora et labora*, meaning 'pray and work'.

As the Middle Ages progressed, monasteries became immensely influential institutions, serving not only as places of prayer and meditation, but also as centres of learning and as providers of charity and basic medical care to their local communities. Monks may have started out wanting to seek God alone in the desert, but they ended up playing a significant role in serving the wider world. In early mediaeval Ireland, for example, monasteries served as centres of missionary activity, sending out missionaries to evangelise pagan peoples – not something that we might initially associate with monks and nuns.

It wasn't unusual for people to leave lands and other bequests to religious orders in their wills or for powerful secular lords to seek out their wisdom and learning. As time went on, many monastic communities therefore grew in prestige and position. Whereas monks and nuns were sworn to poverty, chastity and obedience as individuals (following the example of Acts 2), the communities could collectively become very wealthy and extremely powerful. The temptations of wealth and power can prove very difficult to escape.

However, the demise of monasticism began with the Reformation. Many monasteries, abbeys and nunneries were shut down, their inmates pensioned off and their lands seized by the state or bought by wealthy landowners. It is probably true that a number of these communities had indeed grown corrupt and no longer served their original purposes, as argued by those who sought their end. However, the dissolution of the monasteries had all sorts of unintended social costs for it brought to an end many sources of aid for the poor and vulnerable (a role increasingly filled afterwards by civil authorities from the public purse). This fact was lamented by the early 20th-century journalist, Christian apologist and poet G. K. Chesterton:

The inns of God, where no man paid,
that were the walls of the weak;
The King's Servants ate them all.
And still we did not speak.[37]

Monastic communities, for both men and women, are still around today, mainly within the Catholic and Orthodox communions (although there are a few similar communities among Protestant denominations). However, they are not what they once were.

MONASTICISM AND THE ROLE OF WOMEN

Monasticism provided one of the relatively few opportunities in the ancient and mediaeval worlds for women to exercise positions of authority in the church and the wider society. A good example is that of Hilda of Whitby (614–680), the abbess of a religious community of both men and women near Hartlepool, who was famed for her wisdom. Her community hosted the famous Synod of Whitby, helping to settle a dispute raging between Celtic and Anglo-Saxon Christians, chiefly over the date of Easter.

Another way in which monastic communities enabled women to exercise influence was through their writings. For example, Mother Julian of Norwich (1342–1416) – an anchorite (a type of hermit) – wrote a devotional work, *Revelations of Divine Love,* which is still being read over six centuries later. She is perhaps best known for her vision of a nut, representing all that God made, treasured and cared for. She also often referred to Christ as our mother, reflecting God's loving care for us as children.

Monastic life was comparatively egalitarian compared to that of the wider society in which it operated. Perhaps this is one of the ways in which monasteries served as a prophetic witness to the world.

SUGGESTED APPLICATION

Perhaps the most obvious application from the rise of monasticism is the single-minded devotion shown by many of the monks and nuns (especially in the early days) to following Christ, no matter what the cost to themselves. At their best, monastic communities provided radical examples of Christian living which could encourage and serve those believers who continued to live in the world. Monasticism could thereby act as a prophetic voice against worldliness, lukewarmness and inequality in the church. The Christian life is, after all, a call to die to oneself, take up one's cross and follow Christ. While few, if any, of us will be called to become monks or nuns, it is still worth asking ourselves how we could seek to integrate their commitment to Christ and service to the wider community into our lives today.

QUESTIONS FOR FURTHER STUDY

1 Do you have any experiences of going on a Christian retreat? Did you find this helpful? Why or why not?

2 What is your reaction to reading how Anthony the Great lived out in the desert, away from civilisation?

3 In your view is the decline of monasticism a cause of celebration or regret, or neither, or a bit of both?

4 How can we integrate a radical commitment to Christ and serving our communities into our lives today?

5

A RESTLESS HEART

One man's story is of particular importance in the history of Christianity in the West. He was a restless man, a man who had done many things in his youth which he regretted. One offence which particularly haunted him was the theft of some pears from a neighbour's orchard. He hadn't stolen them because he was hungry or in need, or even because he particularly liked pears, but simply for the enjoyment of committing a crime, and he felt that this was a truer mark of the evil within him than his womanising or hankering after fame. One day, as we shall see, he reached a point of crisis and threw himself upon God's grace. God's grace utterly changed his life, and with it the future of Western Christianity, forever.

This man was Aurelius Augustinus, better known to history as Augustine of Hippo.[38] Without him the mediaeval church would have been radically different, and there may well have been no Protestant Reformation.

AUGUSTINE'S EARLY LIFE AND CONVERSION

Augustine was born in 354 in Tagaste, in modern Tunisia, to a Roman father, Patricius, and an African mother, Monica. Monica was a Christian and faithful in her consistent, fervent prayer for, and testimony to, Augustine over several decades prior to his eventual conversion.

As a young man, Augustine turned away from his Christian upbringing, eventually embracing a dualistic sect called Manichaeism, which saw darkness (and evil) as an eternal and rival principle to light (and good). The Manichees were divided into an outer group, known as the 'hearers', and an inner group called the 'elect', who were expected to exercise rigorous self-control and be both completely celibate and vegetarian. Augustine was a 'hearer', but he was very far from exercising self-mastery in his personal life.

But then Augustine encountered the teaching of one of the great Western fathers of the church, Ambrose, Bishop of Milan (340–397). Ambrose was able to share the Christian faith with Augustine in a way which made sense to him. He became more accepting of Christian teaching, but still felt far from God. Then came a decisive moment of crisis, while Augustine was out walking one day with his friend Alypius. The dramatic nature of his conversion is important in helping us understand the emphasis that Augustine puts on God's initiative and grace. He recounts it as follows:

Now when deep reflection had drawn up out of the secret depths of my soul all my misery and had heaped it up before the sight of my heart, there arose a mighty storm, accompanied by a mighty rain of tears. That I might give way fully to my tears and lamentations, I stole away from Alypius, for it seemed to me that solitude was more appropriate for the business of weeping. I went far enough away that I could feel that even his presence was no restraint upon me. This was the way I felt at the time, and he realised it. I suppose I had said something before I started up and he noticed that the sound of my voice was choked with weeping. And so he stayed alone where we had been sitting together, greatly astonished. I flung myself down under a fig tree – how I knew not – and gave free course to my tears. The streams of my eyes gushed out an acceptable sacrifice to You. And not indeed in these words, but to this effect, I cried to You: 'And You, O Lord, how long? How long, O Lord? Will You be angry forever? Oh remember not against us our former iniquities.' For I felt that I was still enthralled by them. I sent up these sorrowful cries: 'How long, how long? Tomorrow and tomorrow? Why not now? Why not this very hour make an end to my uncleanness?'

I was saying these things and weeping in the most bitter contrition of my heart, when suddenly I heard the voice of a boy or girl – I know not which – coming from the neighbouring house, chanting over and over again, 'Pick it up, read it; pick it up, read it.' Immediately I ceased weeping and began most earnestly to think whether it was usual for children in some kind of game to sing such a song, but I could not ever remember having heard the like. So, damming the torrent of my tears, I got to my feet, for I could not but think that this was a divine command to open the Bible and read the first passage I should light upon. For I had heard how Anthony, accidentally coming into church while the Gospel was being read, received the admonition as if what had been read had been addressed to him: 'Go and sell what you have and give it to the poor, and you shall have treasure in heaven: and come and follow me.' By such an oracle he was forthwith converted to You.[39]

So I quickly returned to the bench where Alypius was sitting, for there I had put down the apostle's book when I had left there. I snatched it up, opened it, and in silence read the paragraph on which my eyes first fell: 'Not in rioting and drunkenness, not in chambering and wantonness, not in strife and envying, but put on the Lord Jesus Christ, and make no provision for the flesh to satisfy the lusts thereof.'[40] *I wanted to read no further, nor did I need to. For instantly the sentence ended, there was infused in my heart something like the light of full certainty and all the gloom of doubt vanished away.*[41]

Following his conversion, Augustine pursued a life of study and contemplation in a community of Christian men. This was a relatively peaceful period in his life, although marred by loss: the death of his mother, Monica, and of his son, Adeodatus.

His autobiographical work, the *Confessions*, shows his later Christian life as being marked by regret over his youthful indulgences. Indeed Augustine is known today for his rather negative view of human nature (especially of human sexuality). It is worth considering, though, how much of his theology was shaped by this 'baggage' of his former life.

AUGUSTINE'S LATER LIFE AND MINISTRY

Augustine's life took a dramatic and unexpected turn in 391. While on a visit to the city of Hippo Regius, in what is now Tunisia – to meet someone thinking about joining his community of Christian men – he was recognised in church by the local bishop. In a departure from his prepared sermon, the bishop stirred up the congregation about the need for new church elders. As a result of this passionate appeal, Augustine was seized and ordained on the spot by the congregation, somewhat against his will. He went on to become first co-bishop and then bishop of the church in Hippo Regius until his death in 430.

In addition to this church role, Augustine produced an astonishing volume of written work: 113 books and over 500 sermons of his survive. One book, *The Retractions*, written near the end of his life, reviews his 93 most important works and takes back those statements in them which he had come to see as being in error. Augustine also engaged in a number of controversies, perhaps the two most important being on the nature of the church and on the nature of God's grace.

CONTROVERSY ONE: AUGUSTINE AND THE CHURCH OF GOD

Augustine's teaching on church membership was largely in response to the arguments of pagans and a group known as the Donatists. It culminated in the publication of one of his most well-known books, *The City of God Against the Pagans*.

Augustine and the Donatists

The Donatists were a Christian community, based in North Africa, who had broken away from the church following the re-admission of backslidden Christians who had denied their faith during persecution. They wanted nothing to do with those who had betrayed the Lord in this way, and sought to build a pure church, unsullied by compromise with the world. For the Donatists there was no promise of redemption for those who had fallen so far.

While there were a number of such groups in the early church, the Donatists stood out from the crowd because of their belief that the validity of the sacraments was linked to the worthiness (or otherwise) of the person who performed them. In other words, if the person who had baptised you turned out to be a fraud or a criminal, then you might not really be baptised after all! In his short book *On Baptism, Against the Donatists*, Augustine accepts that genuine baptism can exist among the Donatists – regardless of the purity of the person conducting the ceremony. But the Donatists themselves seem to have been pickier, choosing to re-baptise converts to their movement.

One important outcome of the Donatist controversy was that it set a precedent within the Catholic Church for accepting baptisms by other Christians as valid. This is significant when considering more recent moves towards greater Christian unity. The Eastern Orthodox churches, by contrast, have tended not to follow Augustine's logic here. Despite this though, it isn't that uncommon for converts to Eastern Orthodoxy from other churches to be welcomed in through prayer or through anointing with oil (a process known as 'chrismation') without having to be baptised all over again.

There is another legacy to this dispute, however, which isn't quite so positive. As a well-known African bishop, Augustine played a major part in trying to bring Donatists back into communion with the rest of the church in North Africa. Unfortunately, his attempts to do so involved him agreeing with the idea that coercion could be used to bring the Donatists back in line.[42] In support of this view he quoted (though many would argue misquoted) Luke 14:23: 'compel them to come in', implying that this recourse to force was alright. It is extremely ironic to find the church, which had only fairly recently been on the receiving end of official persecution, now encouraging government officials to use force against splitters within its own ranks!

Augustine and the City of God

Among Augustine's best-known books was *The City of God Against the Pagans*. This great work was begun in 413 and finally published in 426, only four years before Augustine's own death. It is significant in the development of Christian understanding of the church (at least in the West). The book was initially written to counter the accusation that the successful attack on Rome by the Goths in 410 could be blamed on the abandonment of the old pagan gods for the new (and supposedly weak) religion of Christianity. In response Augustine argues that Rome had always faced calamities and that the pagan gods, far from protecting the city, were at best non-entities and at worst deluding demonic spirits, who couldn't even protect their own shrines!

The City of God contains 22 books and its argument ranges far beyond its original purpose. Augustine tends to wander from the point (to put it mildly), sometimes making his argument hard to follow. Yet the main point of the work is to contrast two 'cities' – the heavenly and the earthly – which differ from one another on the basis of what their citizens love. As Augustine puts it: 'Two cities, then, have been created by two loves: that is, the earthly by love of self, extending even to contempt of God, and the heavenly by love of God, extending to contempt of self.'[43]

Augustine held a very exalted view of the institutional church as the body of Christ, but even he didn't believe that all who are members of the institutional church are necessarily thereby citizens of the City of God. Neither did he believe that all who are outside the institutional church (such as those who lived and believed under the Old Testament) were therefore necessarily outside the heavenly city. This interpretation points in a similar direction to the later Protestant idea of a 'visible' church (namely, the church as an institution) and an 'invisible' church (composed of all true believers in heaven and earth).

CONTROVERSY TWO: AUGUSTINE AND THE GRACE OF GOD

One of the titles given to Augustine is that of *doctor gratiae* (a Latin term meaning 'teacher of grace'). God's grace was a prominent theme in his teaching.

It is important, though, to be clear as to the meaning of this term. In the New Testament, the word 'grace' is a translation of the Greek word *charis*. This has quite a wide range of meanings from 'favour' and 'goodwill' to 'gratitude' and 'thanks'. (As we saw in chapter two, the Lord's Supper was sometimes called the Eucharist – the giving of thanks). Grace can also be defined as 'a special manifestation of the divine presence, activity, power or glory'.[44] Reference to God's grace, then, is not only about his goodness to undeserving people (the usual evangelical understanding) but also a supernatural ability. Grace is not simply God's pardon but also God's power and God's presence.

Augustine and Pelagius

Augustine's teachings on the grace of God came about largely as a reaction to the teachings of a man named Pelagius, a British-born moralist. Little is known about Pelagius prior to 400, although he does appear to have lived in Rome for a time.

Pelagius's emphasis on self-control and a strong belief in human free-will led him to deny that the sin of Adam had caused any negative effect at all on subsequent generations except as a bad example or precedent. According to Pelagius, therefore, all human beings were born morally neutral, without any taint of sin. In his view salvation consisted of following the counteracting good example set by Christ. As a result, God's grace, while extremely helpful, was not strictly necessary.

What particularly seems to have offended Pelagius was Augustine's idea that our obedience to God is something that God himself gives us. Pelagius was especially scandalised by Augustine's assertion that when we speak to God, we should say: 'Give what You command, and command what You will.'[45]

In response to this, Augustine argued that the sin of Adam caused the fall of the entire human race, putting us all beyond hope of salvation unless God intervenes by being gracious to us. He says of God's grace: 'This mercy is prevenient to [that is, it goes ahead of] the unwilling to make him will; it follows the willing that he may not will in vain.'[46] In other words, according to Augustine, we need God to give us grace before conversion, so that we want to turn to him and be saved. We also need God to keep on giving us grace after we have turned to him for salvation, so that we continue to look to him and stay saved.

Original sin and the baptism of babies

The issue of infant baptism features heavily in this debate between Augustine and Pelagius. Pelagius, who himself believed in baptising babies, found it difficult to explain his viewpoint since he alleged babies had no original sin to wash away. Augustine's logic was at the other extreme (much to the horror of subsequent generations, and to himself). He taught that since all babies are born guilty of sin committed in Adam, and since baptism is necessary to wash their sins away, then all babies who die unbaptised must therefore be damned to hell for sinning in Adam.

This view was softened by later generations, who conceived of a *limbus infantum* (literally, a 'borderland of babies', commonly known as 'Limbo') at the outskirts of hell. They believed that unbaptised babies who had died in infancy would go to Limbo, thus being excluded from heaven and the vision of God, but experiencing no further suffering. Yet even in this milder form, such teaching supported the trend away from delaying baptism until old age and towards the baptism of young babies.

This is, understandably, a very difficult subject for some. It is therefore perhaps worth noting that the opinions of Augustine and Pelagius were not the only two views on this issue. The Eastern view opposed both the Pelagian teaching as well as what was seen as Augustine's over-reaction to it. In essence Eastern Christians held (and continue to hold) the idea that no one is born guilty of the sin of Adam – thus being in opposition to Augustine. Likewise they maintained that the sin of Adam introduced death, defilement and weakness into the world – in opposition to Pelagius's teaching. In their view unbaptised babies who died in infancy have no personal guilt for the sin of Adam (see Ezekiel 18), but are nonetheless inevitably wounded and weakened by it, growing up to be sinners.

A good way of understanding these two views of original sin is that Western Christianity tends to see original sin as a capital crime while Eastern Christianity tends to see it more as a mortal wound or a terminal disease. The distinction between these two perspectives on sin is just one of the many ways in which Eastern and Western Christianity drifted apart from each other before their final separation (see the next chapter).

Semi-Pelagianism

A variant of Pelagius's teaching (known by later generations as Semi-Pelagianism) arose just before Augustine's death. This asserted that while sinners cannot be saved without the help of God's grace co-operating with them, they are still able to, as it were, set the ball rolling towards salvation by their own efforts. However, their viewpoint was rejected by the Second Council of Orange, in 529, who argued that what theologians call prevenient grace (the grace which goes before human choice) is necessary for salvation. This council also strongly condemned 'predestination to evil' (a form of double predestination)[47] and taught that the initial grace which enables us to co-operate with God is received through baptism.

THE LEGACY OF AUGUSTINE

Augustine of Hippo remains a major influence on Western Christianity. Both Catholics and Protestants quoted his works as being authoritative during the debates of the Reformation in the 16th century. For example, the writings of Augustine are the second most widely quoted authority in John Calvin's *Institutes of the Christian Religion* (a key text of the Protestant Reformation), taking second place only to the Bible itself. In light of this, and given his strong focus on God's grace, a good case can be made that without Augustine there would have been no Reformation at all! Yet the 'blessed Augustine' (as he is sometimes known in the East) is far less influential as a theologian among Eastern Orthodox Christians.

In addition, Augustine has influenced general Western thought. For example, his autobiographical work, *The Confessions*, is arguably the first book of its type. Augustine lived at the beginning of the end of the Western Roman Empire and his writing helps to link the thought of the classical and mediaeval eras. His works also largely survived in the West, while many others were lost following the fall of Roman authority, and this inevitably increased his influence.

SUGGESTED APPLICATIONS

There are many ways in which we could seek to learn from Augustine's life. His understanding of the phrase 'compel them to come in' and its tragic consequences teaches us to be careful before expressing what we think or feel, especially if we find ourselves in a position to teach or influence others. In a similar vein, it might also be worth reflecting how much our own past experiences can shape our current thoughts and ideas. How much are our beliefs affected by our baggage?

Augustine's *Retractions* – his review of his writings near the end of his life, in which he takes back statements he considered mistaken – teaches us the importance of being able to say that we were wrong. Augustine was a great figure in Christian history, but he wasn't above being able to admit his errors. Perhaps we might wish that he had changed his mind in different ways than he did, but the fact that he was able to criticise himself is one of the better examples he has left us.

Most of all, though, it is Augustine's sense of our utter dependence on the mercy and enabling power of God that is, perhaps, his greatest lesson to us. (This issue will come up again when we look at the Calvinist–Arminian dispute in a later chapter.) Those who have come to faith in Christ have done so because God's mercy has gone ahead of them to lead them to him. Those who remain faithful to Christ do so because God's grace comes alongside them, enabling them to remain in the faith. As the New Testament would teach us, 'it is by grace you have been saved' (Ephesians 2:5 and 8).

QUESTIONS FOR FURTHER STUDY

1 Can you think of any example from your own life where your beliefs or actions have been influenced by baggage from the past?

2 Have you ever retracted something that you've said or written? If so, what caused you to change your mind?

3 How can we better seek to live our lives in dependence upon God's grace?

6

TORN APART

'How good and how pleasant it is when God's people live together in unity!' (Psalm 133:1). Disunity and conflict between believers is a stumbling block for many considering the claims of Christ. Why can't we agree on what we believe to be true? Alas, these divisions are not new. The First Council of Nicaea tried to unify the church, but disagreements continued – as they continue today. Together with misunderstandings, over-reactions, rivalries and sordid scheming, they tore Christianity apart. In the fifth century, a large group of churches broke away. In the 11th century, Christianity as a whole was torn in half to form two rival groups of churches.

NESTORIUS AND EUTYCHES

One of the most significant theological disagreements within the early church concerned the relationship between the divinity and the humanity of Christ. The church had (largely) agreed that Christ is divine in the same way that God the Father is divine – contrary to the teaching of Arius (see chapter three). The church had also established that Christ really became a human being – in contrast to the beliefs of the Gnostics and their ilk. This left the question as to how the divine nature of Christ and the human nature of Christ related to one another.

In the early fifth century, Nestorius, the Bishop of Constantinople, began to teach that the Virgin Mary ought not to be called the *Theotokos*, or 'Mother of God', but rather the *Christotokos*, or 'Mother of Christ', arguing that it was impossible for God to have been born from a human being. Nestorius emphasised the fact that Christ was a real man, born from a real woman. Yet in doing so, he seemed to divide the human being, Jesus of Nazareth, from the second person of the Trinity, although he did argue that the two were 'conjoined'. This teaching led to heated disputes and accusations that the Nestorians separated Christ's humanity from his divinity, although this was probably not entirely fair, at least as far as Nestorius himself was concerned.

At the other end of the spectrum was the teaching of a monk named Eutyches. Whereas the Nestorians seemed to over-distinguish Christ's divinity and humanity, Eutyches blended them together to form a composite human–divine nature, neither fully human nor fully divine (similar to the way that spring is neither winter nor summer). The problem with Eutychianism (as it became known) was that it effectively lost both the divinity and the humanity of Christ.

Since many in the early church believed that God becoming a human being in Christ is what enables people to be saved, they didn't want to subscribe to a teaching which divided Christ's divinity and humanity from each other. Yet neither did they desire to embrace an alternative which blended them together to form something in between.

CHALCEDON

The Council of Chalcedon met in 451 to look at this dispute. It affirmed its belief in the Nicene Creed and attached an appendix (known as the Definition of Chalcedon) that sought to define the relationship between the divine nature and the human nature of Christ, and which runs as follows:

> *We then, following the holy Fathers, all with one accord teach people to confess one and the same Son, our Lord Jesus Christ, at once perfect in divinity and perfect in humanity, truly God and truly human, consisting also of a rational soul and body; of one being with the Father as regards his divinity, and at the same time of one being with us as regards his humanity, like us in all respects, apart from sin. As regards his divinity, begotten of the Father before all ages, but yet as regards his humanity, begotten, for us human beings and for our salvation, of Mary the Virgin, the Mother of God; one and the same Christ, Son, Lord, Only-begotten, recognized in two natures, without confusion, without change, without division, without separation; the distinction of natures being in no way taken away by the union, but rather*

> *the characteristics of each nature being preserved and coming together in one person and one subsistence, not as parted or separated into two persons, but one and the same Son and Only-begotten, God the Word, Lord Jesus Christ, even as the prophets from the beginning have declared concerning him and our Lord Jesus Christ himself taught us, and the creed of the holy Fathers has handed down to us.* (My translation).

In other words, the Council of Chalcedon declared that Jesus Christ, the Son of God, who has come down to us in human form, is both 100% divine and 100% human.

Unfortunately, though, this definition failed to achieve unity, as a number of believers in the East – concerned that the 'two natures in one person' formula came too close to the Nestorian teaching – broke away to form their own churches. They became known as monophysites (from the Greek meaning 'only one nature'). Some of these breakaway groups exist today, including the Ethiopian Orthodox churches and the Egyptian Copts (two of the oldest Christian churches in Africa), although these churches would not necessarily regard the term 'monophysite' as being an accurate description of what they believe.

More recent discussions have taken place between these churches and those which accepted the Definition of Chalcedon, and the two sides are closer to reaching a common understanding than they have been for many centuries. Nevertheless, the breaking away of these Eastern Christian groups[48] was a blow to the church, since it effectively separated many of the churches in Egypt and Ethiopia (and some others further east) from the rest of Christianity. Moreover, even worse divisions were to come.

THE FALL OF ROME AND A NEW EMPIRE

The attacks on the city of Rome by the Goths in 410 and by the Vandals[49] around 455 marked the beginning of the end of the Western Roman Empire. The fall of the empire was a cataclysmic event. Yet, while much of the West was overrun with barbarians, the Catholic Church survived. It was the inheritor of Roman culture and learning. Furthermore, the power of the pope[50] and the bishops grew as the church stepped in to fill the gap. Christendom rose on the ruins of Rome's power. People in the West, who had once been united as Romans, came to find common identity as Christians. In the East, by contrast, imperial authority continued for another thousand years or so, in the form of the Eastern Roman (or Byzantine) Empire.

In the eighth century a new Western empire came into being. Charles the Great (724–814), also known as Charlemagne, united France, Germany and northern Italy into a single territory. This unity brought relative peace to Western Europe for long enough that various schools of learning and a great library in Aachen (in Germany) could come into being. Though after Charlemagne's death the empire's territory soon became largely confined to what is now Germany and Austria, this new 'Holy Roman Empire of the German Nation' was to survive for around a thousand years.

GROWING APART

In 1054 Christianity was finally torn apart in the Great Schism to form two separate, rival Christian churches: East and West; Orthodox and Catholic. The first key to understanding why this happened can be found in some of the ways in which the Western Christians had grown apart from their brothers and sisters in the East.

In extremely general terms, the Eastern tendency is to emphasise the unknowability of God whereas the Western tendency is to emphasise what can be known about God. (However, this distinction between the 'mystical' East and the 'rational' West can be overstated). Likewise, Western Christianity did (and does) place a greater emphasis on legal and judicial metaphors for salvation than in the East, where the emphasis is more on healing from the disease of sin and restoring fallen humanity to the image of God. As we also saw in chapter five, the East holds a different view of the Fall of Adam and original sin than that which Augustine taught in the West. For Eastern Christians it is not that human nature itself has fallen (otherwise how could Christ have become human?) but that we as people have fallen from our human nature, as God intended it to be.

Other misunderstandings arose through language barriers. One good example concerns the Trinity. What do you call the 'one-ness' of God and what do you call the 'three-ness' of God? To the Greek-speakers in the East, God was one *ousia* (being) in three *hypostases* (subsistences). To the Latin-speakers in the West, God was one *substantia* (substance) in three *personae* (persons). Yet the problem here was that the Latin word *substantia* is essentially equivalent to the Greek word *hypostasis* (both coming from root words meaning 'under' and 'stand'). In other words, the term used by one side to refer to the 'one-ness' of God could be used by the other for his 'three-ness'. With language barriers like these, Eastern and Western believers could easily sound like heretics to each other, even when they were saying the same thing!

POLITICAL CONSIDERATIONS

Another factor in the Great Schism was the political scene. The rise of Islam had led to many of the important churches in the East, such as the churches of Antioch, Alexandria and Jerusalem, coming under Islamic rule. This strengthened the position of the Patriarch of Constantinople (in what is now Istanbul), who, as the most senior Christian figure in the East not living under Islamic rule, became the leading bishop among Eastern Christians. As such he became a potential rival to the pope in Rome, to whom Western churches held allegiance and whose political position, as we have seen, grew in strength as the Western Empire collapsed.

This was compounded by the political division between the East and West. This wasn't a new problem: the emperor Diocletian had divided the Roman Empire into East and West, each with its own emperor. Constantine the Great had reunited the empire under himself but this new unity didn't last. While the leadership of the church remained united, however, it didn't matter so much whether there were one or two emperors. However, the situation changed when the Holy Roman Empire of Charlemagne rose in the place of the Western Roman Empire. This time there were two emperors, the Eastern Roman (or Byzantine) Emperor in Constantinople and the new Holy Roman Emperor in Germany in the West, allied to two rival Christian leaders: the Patriarch of Constantinople and the pope in Rome. This political and religious rivalry did not help the two sides in maintaining unity and a common understanding of the faith.

THE FILIOQUE CONTROVERSY

The final split came about as a result of something called the *Filioque* controversy. The word *Filioque* is Latin for 'and from the Son'. These words were added to the final paragraph of the Nicene Creed by the Third Council of Toledo (in Spain) in 589. Therefore, whereas the Eastern (and original) text of the Creed said that the Holy Spirit 'proceeds from the Father', the Western version of the creed taught that the Holy Spirit 'proceeds from the Father and the Son'. (It wasn't until 1014, though, that this longer wording was used in Rome.) Many Eastern Christians, however, fundamentally disagreed with these extra words, for the following reasons.

Firstly, many in the East argued that teaching that the Holy Spirit proceeds from both the Father and the Son was wrong in itself. Their main objection seems to have been that the teaching denied the unique role of the Father as the eternal source of the Trinity, thus seemingly contradicting the teaching agreed by the church at Nicaea. Furthermore, they maintained that saying the Spirit proceeds from both the Father and the Son could be understood as implying that the Spirit was somehow less than the Son.

Secondly, the *Filioque* clause was rejected because, from the standpoint of the East, neither a provincial church council in Spain nor even the pope in Rome had the authority to add anything to the creed. Thus, regardless of whether the doctrine itself was orthodox or not, the split was also largely a dispute about the authority of the pope.

In response, Western Christians argued that stating that the Spirit also proceeds from the Son was necessary to emphasise that the Son is also fully God. Arianism had made a comeback in the West following the fall of Rome to the Goths (who were largely Arians) and needed to be countered. It was this need to show that Jesus is also fully God that prompted the church leaders in Toledo to add these extra words in the first place. Another argument for the *Filioque* wording is that it helps to show that there is a relationship between the Son and the Holy Spirit within the Trinity.

While it took some time before the *Filioque* phrase was added to the Nicene Creed, it had been used in the West in the so-called 'Athanasian Creed' from the fifth century. There were also some early church fathers in the West (such as Tertullian and Augustine) who had used similar wording when talking about the relationship between the

Son and the Holy Spirit. After all, the Holy Spirit is also called the 'Spirit of Christ' (Romans 8:9).

Clearly it is vital to establish what the Bible says on this. The key text for understanding the dispute is John 15:26: 'When the Advocate comes, whom I will send (*pempsō*) to you from the Father – the Spirit of truth who goes out (*ekporeuetai*) from the Father – he will testify about me' (Greek text added). As you can see, the Greek word for the Spirit being sent by Christ is different from the Greek word for the Spirit going out (or proceeding) from the Father. This could imply that a distinction should be made between the way in which the Trinity operates in eternity (what theologians call the 'imminent' or 'ontological' Trinity) and the way in which the Trinity chooses to operate in relation to saving the world (what theologians call the 'economic' Trinity).

This distinction could prove fruitful in bringing both sides to a common understanding of the question. Indeed the churches are much closer to resolving this dispute than was the case back in 1054. The idea that the Holy Spirit proceeds from the Father *through* the Son goes back at least as far as Tertullian in the third century, and appears to be acceptable to both sides. There have also been calls for the Nicene Creed to be read in churches in its original form (without the *Filioque*) so that both sides can use a common text.

THE IMPACT AND LEGACY OF THE SCHISM

However, even if this theological dispute were to be resolved – as looks plausible – there is still disagreement on other issues, not least the role and power of the pope. Furthermore, resolving the theological question does not, by itself, erase the painful legacy of horrific acts committed by both sides, including during the Crusades, which we shall look at in the next chapter.

The Great Schism divided both Christianity and the continent of Europe into two, with Eastern and Western Christians going their separate ways. The fact that much of the Eastern Church came under first Islamic and later Communist rule also helped in the alienation of the two traditions. Even now, talks between East and West are hindered by the different histories and perspectives of the two sides.

SUGGESTED APPLICATIONS

At times theology can be hard to grasp. However, surely that in itself is a lesson: Christian belief doesn't involve sidelining your brain, as some allege, but instead can involve hard thinking, especially about matters which are controversial or cause disunity. After all, Jesus urges us: 'Love the Lord your God with all your … mind' (Matthew 22:37).

Another lesson to take away is the importance of rightly understanding one another. You could write a book of Christian history based almost entirely around how groups within Christianity either misunderstood one another or else over-reacted to something that the 'other side' said (or that they thought that they had said). Yes, truth is important; it is good to be zealous for the truth. But our model here should be the Lord Jesus himself who is 'full of grace and truth' (John 1:14). Showing grace to others should surely involve finding out what they are really trying to say before we embark on expounding why they are wrong.

QUESTIONS FOR FURTHER STUDY

1. Can you spot which lines in the Definition of Chalcedon refer to the Nestorians and which to the Eutychians?
2. Before reading this chapter, had you heard of the *Filioque* controversy? If so, has reading this chapter changed your view of it in any way?
3. How can we avoid misunderstandings and over-reactions?
4. What else can we do as individuals to help promote greater Christian unity?

7

HOLY WAR

In November 1095, Pope Urban II preached a powerful sermon in Clermont. In it he described, in graphic detail, a number of horrific atrocities which had allegedly been committed by Muslims against Christian pilgrims in the Holy Land. Appealing to their honour (and perhaps also to their self-interest), he called upon the brave warriors of Christian Europe to intervene, to defeat Islam and to capture Jerusalem under the sign of the cross. Coming as it did at the end of a long papal tour, this was an electrifying message. The response of the audience was to cry out in Latin, '*Deus vult!*' ('God wills it!'). So began the series of Western military interventions in the Middle East known to history as the Crusades.

THE REASONS FOR THE CRUSADES

But why were the Crusades thought to be necessary? And, perhaps just as puzzling, why now? Jerusalem had been under Muslim rule for centuries by the time Pope Urban II gave this speech. What prompted such urgency?

The official reason for the war was a request by the Emperor of the Byzantine (or Eastern Roman) Empire in Constantinople (modern-day Istanbul) for some military assistance from his Christian brothers in the West to help them defend themselves against attacking Turkish armies. However, the Eastern Christians were fundamentally opposed to holy war and only seem to have expected a few thousand knights to turn up, not tens of thousands of holy warriors! The underlying causes perhaps lay closer to home.

At the end of the 11th century, Western Europe was riven with conflict, Christian ruler fighting Christian ruler. A war against Islam could serve to unite the West. Furthermore, in the aftermath of the Great Schism (which we looked at in the previous chapter), there was a desire to heal the divisions within Christianity.

On a more individual level, the incentives for people to go on crusade were powerful indeed. Those who took up the cross were (wrongly) promised forgiveness for all their sins, which is why so many of the crusaders seem to have had dubious pasts. After having first been required to confess all their misdeeds, a crusade supposedly served as a penance, or act of repentance, for those who went. Those who died on crusade would die as martyrs. Furthermore, in a time when harvests had repeatedly failed, the promise of a journey to a land supposedly flowing with milk and honey was a welcome one indeed. It also shouldn't be forgotten that 11th-century Europe was a very honour-centred culture, especially for the military class. Many of those who heard Pope Urban's appeal would have felt honour-bound to respond.

A HISTORY OF THE CRUSADES

From a military perspective, the First Crusade was a resounding success, at least for those on the crusader side. A number of cities were captured, including, most importantly, the city of Jerusalem. This victory, however, was marred by atrocity with the subsequent massacre of civilians. Other awful events took place elsewhere, though the massacre in Jerusalem was perhaps the worst. Together they would be used to justify many other outrages in later years: both acts of retaliation by Muslims, as we shall see, as well as further atrocities by crusaders, for whom these early massacres set a grim precedent.

The capture of the Holy Land by the crusaders led to the establishment of several crusader territories, including Antioch (a key city in the history of the early church), Edessa and, of course, the Kingdom of Jerusalem. Christian churches and shrines were adorned. Nevertheless, Islamic holy sites, such as the Al-Aqsa Mosque, remained, and both Christians and Muslims continued to travel on pilgrimage.

During the later decades of relative peace, Queen Melissande of Jerusalem gained repute as a notable ruler, having been crowned as joint-monarch with her husband and son in 1131 – a highly unusual arrangement for the time and not much to her husband's liking, it would seem. She ruled after his death as a competent and respected leader, eventually giving way to her son, although even then retaining much of her power.

This relative peace, however, was not to last long. The capture and virtual destruction of the city of Edessa by an Islamic ruler, Zengi of Aleppo, led to the Second Crusade being called in 1145 by Pope Eugenius III. The crusading message still had power on hearts and minds across Europe. One of the great Christian teachers of the age, Abbot Bernard of Clairvaux, travelled widely, using his powerful preaching to whip up support for the new crusade.

Of course, none of this enthusiasm guaranteed military success. The crusaders suffered a humiliating defeat outside the walls of Damascus. There was worse news for them still to come when, in 1187, the great sultan Salah al-Din Yusuf ibn Ayyub (better known in the West as Saladin) recaptured Jerusalem for Islam.

Christian Europe responded with a Third Crusade, perhaps the best known of them all. The conflict between Saladin and his opponent, Richard II ('the Lionheart') of England,[51] is the stuff of legend. Yet this later crusade didn't retake Jerusalem either – none of them did. Though the city briefly returned to Christian rule in 1229 under Emperor Frederick II, this was more of a diplomatic triumph[52] than a military one, and the new Christian ruler was technically excommunicated from the Catholic Church at the time. Jerusalem was again in Muslim hands in 1244 and would remain so for the next six centuries.

Later crusades were called, often attempting to attack via Egypt, but to no avail. Eventually, in 1291, the last crusader-controlled city in the Middle East, the city of Acre (on the Israeli coast), fell and its inhabitants were brutally massacred, as the inhabitants of Jerusalem had been in 1099 when the Crusades began.

As we have already noted, though, for many of those who took part in these conflicts, they were intended to be temporary affairs. People went on crusade to obtain forgiveness for their sins, or to gain honour, fame or wealth. Once a crusade was over, many crusaders returned home, leaving relatively few people behind to defend captured territories. This fact may help to explain why they were ultimately so unsuccessful.

THE DIVERSITY OF THE CRUSADES

Crusades didn't only take place in the Middle East, though. The Second Crusade, for example, included wars in Spain and Portugal against the Muslim population there, as well as a crusade against pagans in the Baltic. These also received the blessing and preaching support of Abbot Bernard, despite church teaching against forced conversion. It would seem that it was thought that nothing says 'Jesus loves you' more than a 'Christian' army turning up, killing your relatives, forcibly seizing your lands and then forcing you to convert, or else!

The Fourth Crusade, perhaps the most disastrous of them all, even led to an attack by crusaders on Constantinople – one of the foremost Christian cities of the

East! Like many others before it, this crusade was originally intended to recapture Jerusalem. It never got there. Instead, it got itself badly indebted to the Venetian republic, whose help the crusaders had sought in obtaining transport to Egypt. A way out of this dilemma appeared when Alexius, a deposed Byzantine prince seeking an empire, promised lavish rewards to the crusaders in return for their help in putting him on the imperial throne in Constantinople. Thus the crusade was diverted there. What was initially a reasonably disciplined attack in support of Alexius soon descended into a wretched orgy of murder, looting and sacrilege – the Sack of Constantinople in 1204. Crusaders despoiled churches and robbed houses, and a prostitute danced on the altar of the Hagia Sophia, the main church of the city, in front of drunken onlookers.

Even Pope Innocent III, a fanatical supporter of the Crusades, who at first had welcomed the East being brought under papal rule, was appalled when the full details became known. This crusade of Christian against Christian, however unintended at the beginning, remains to this day an open wound in attempts to reconcile the Eastern and Western churches.

Nevertheless, in 1209 Pope Innocent III called another crusade, this time not to the Middle East nor to Constantinople, but to southern France. The Albigensian Crusade, as it is known, was directed against a group called the Cathars ('pure ones'). Like the Gnostics and Manichees of old, they taught a dualism between the sinful material world and a pure ascetic spirituality. This crusade was therefore intended to capture cities in the South of France known to harbour Cathars and their supporters.

Of course this raised a difficulty in the minds of some crusaders. How would they know that they were not killing the faithful along with the heretics? The terrifying answer came from the mouth of the papal representative, Abbot Arnold Almaric, outside the walls of Béziers: 'Kill them all. God will know his own!' Sadly massacre and the seizure of lands was followed by inquisition. Even then, Catharism took a long time to die.

THE LEGACIES OF THE CRUSADES

One immediate legacy of the Crusades was the rise of military orders, such as the Knights Templar, which combined monasticism with military service. Many of these orders have now gone. In the case of the Templars, they were destroyed by King Philip IV of France (1285–1316) on charges – possibly trumped up – of heresy. Nevertheless, the idea of the Christian warrior has lasted, for example, in the 19th-century hymn 'Onward Christian soldiers' and in patriotic Christian sermons during the First World War.

A more obvious and negative legacy of the Crusades is the lasting suspicion, even hatred, between Christians and Muslims that these events fuelled. Modern Western armies, especially armies engaged in conflict in the Middle East, are often referred to by Jihadists (and others) as 'crusader' armies. This lingering mutual resentment is not only confined to Christian–Muslim relations; it also appears, from time to time, as a factor in the ongoing division between Eastern and Western Christians which we looked at in the previous chapter.

Another unpleasant aspect of the Crusades was that many of them included outbreaks of violence against Jewish communities. The first of these attacks, which took place in the Rhineland in 1096 as the crusaders made their way eastwards, was particularly savage. A number of allegations were made against the Jews, the main one being their supposed role as 'Christ-killers'. (Of course, since Christ died for all our sins, aren't we all responsible for his death?) Other charges related to Jewish involvement in usury – the charging of interest on loans. This practice was forbidden to Christians (as being sinful) yet (being useful) was permitted for Jews (who couldn't legally own land and thus often had to earn a living through finance). Jews in mediaeval Europe supposedly lived under royal protection. Sadly, though, once violence had broken out with these attacks, it often took some time before the authorities regained control.

SUGGESTED APPLICATIONS

What does this unhappy period of church history have to teach us? An obvious lesson is that events have consequences, many of which still resonate today. The deeds and choices of the crusaders have not been forgotten, nor do people just 'get over' such incidents. Furthermore, given the appalling things that happened during this period of history, Christians would be wise to be wary about using the word 'crusade' in describing outreach events. It carries huge amounts of emotive, historical and cultural baggage, not only for Muslims but also for Jews, Eastern Christians and others.

Perhaps a good question for us to ask ourselves, in light of these events, is: what do we want our legacy as individuals and as a generation to be? We may be filled with zeal and fervour to do something great for God. This is a noble aim but it is also one which has so often been used as an excuse for great evil. The memory of the Crusades, while unpleasant, may serve as a reminder of this.

QUESTIONS FOR FURTHER STUDY

1 Have you ever referred to a Christian outreach (or any other event) as a crusade?

2 Can you think of any ways in which the crusaders' core ideas are alive today?

3 Do you think that there is any other way that Christians now can learn from the Crusades?

4 What would you wish your legacy to be?

8

MEDIAEVAL WISDOM

At school I learned how Christopher Columbus was very nearly dissuaded from making his epic sea voyage across the Atlantic by mediaeval churchmen, who believed that the world was flat and that he risked falling off the edge. I was an agnostic at the time and this story had great appeal for me, since it demonstrated clearly the triumph of modern scientific reason over mediaeval superstition. It was only much later in life that I found out that there was something wrong with the story – it wasn't actually true.

Now, I'm not accusing my teachers of deliberately lying to me – they had probably been taught the same thing themselves. It is in fact a fairly widely held idea. (I've even seen it being used in TV adverts for beer!) It also chimes with what people think when they hear the term 'Middle Ages'.

Given the Crusades, this negative view of mediaeval Europe is perhaps not a surprise. Was there ignorance[53] and brutality? Undoubtedly yes. However, there is another side to mediaeval Christendom: one which helped lay the foundations of many of the scientific, academic and social achievements of later generations, but which tends to be forgotten or even ignored.

THE MEDIAEVAL UNIVERSE

In mediaeval universities (in which the church played a significant role), one major text that was used to teach students about the physical universe was the *Almagest*. This was written in the early second century by the Egyptian astronomer Claudius Ptolemy, and demonstrates, among other things, that the world is 'sensibly spherical'[54] (that is, that it can be perceived even by the senses to be round) because the sun and moon do not rise (or appear to rise) at the same time for everyone. Not only does Ptolemy demonstrate that the world is round, he also goes on to show that the universe is very big indeed. He does this by noting that astronomers' observations could not be what they were if the earth were of any 'perceptible size in relation to the distance of the heavenly bodies'.[55] This ancient wisdom was preserved by both Christians and Muslims, and became standard teaching in the later mediaeval period, long before Columbus.

There were, nevertheless, a few people who insisted that the Bible taught that the world was flat – the best known of these was the sixth-century traveller and map-maker Cosmas Indicopleustes. His teachings were dragged out of relative obscurity during the 19th-century 'conflict' between science and religion, as though he was somehow representative of

Christian thinking on the subject. However, many leading Christian thinkers of the Middle Ages, including such names as the Venerable Bede (673–735), Roger Bacon (c. 1214–1294) and the poet Dante Alighieri (1265–1321), clearly knew that the earth is a sphere.

So, then, it would seem that Columbus's dispute with the authorities wasn't about whether or not he was going to fall off the edge of the world, after all. What, then, was the issue? It concerned whether the sea was too wide to cross. Columbus's calculation of the circumference of the earth followed that of Claudius Ptolemy, which was rather on the small side. The authorities argued in favour of the measurement of another ancient writer, Erastothenes, who came up with a larger number and one much closer to the truth. While neither side believed Columbus was going to fall off the edge of the world, had he not accidentally bumped into South America, he and his crew would probably have starved to death long before they ever reached land.

In conclusion, mediaeval Christians knew that the earth was round and that the universe was very big indeed. It was only much more recently that either of these truths (and Christians supposed ignorance of them) were used in arguments against Christianity.

THE MEDIAEVAL UNIVERSITY

One of the most important developments of the mediaeval period was the rise of the university. There had been famous schools of learning in the past, generally founded by rulers or by famous teachers and their disciples. The mediaeval university, by contrast, was set up as a guild or corporation of scholars. This gave it a measure of autonomy and enabled it to survive as an entity independently of the scholars who taught and studied in it. Some universities from this early period survive today.

It is difficult to overstate the importance of the development of the university as an autonomous body of scholars, nor how little progress would have been made without it. These universities were the training grounds for new generations of Christian scholars, known as the Scholastics (or 'Schoolmen'). They strove to understand and explain Christian beliefs using reason and logic.[56] The following are among these famous thinkers.

Anselm of Canterbury (1033–1109) developed reasoned arguments for the existence of God. He also developed a new understanding of the significance of Christ's death – that Christ made a satisfaction payment to the Father for the dishonour to him caused by human rebellion – which is not dissimilar to the view held by many evangelicals today.

Peter Abelard (1079–1142) sought to demonstrate all belief by reason and believed in asking difficult questions. It was Abelard who first started using logic to help work out theological problems. However, he was an outspoken man with a tendency to set himself up in opposition to authority and got into all sorts of trouble, not least in his personal life. He is perhaps best known for having a relationship with one of his students, a young woman named Héloïse. Not only was this a terrible idea but also it ended badly: Héloïse was forced into becoming a nun and her enraged family had Abelard castrated by a gang of ruffians! Despite this, Abelard and Héloïse kept in touch, writing letters to each other often throughout their lives. They were buried side by side in Paris.

Thomas Aquinas (1225–1274) sought to reconcile Christian theology and the thought of the ancient Greek philosopher Aristotle. Aristotle's writings had largely been lost to Western Europe after the fall of Rome but his work was widely read and commented on by Islamic scholars. Aquinas wasn't afraid to draw on the work of some of these scholars, notably Ibn-Siīnā (980–1037, known in Latin as Avicenna) and Ibn-Rushd (1126–1198, known in Latin as Averroes), in reclaiming Aristotle for the West. Aquinas created probably the greatest masterpiece of mediaeval Christian theology, the *Summa Theologica* ('Theological Summary'),[57] which remains an important text today. Interestingly, though, the *Summa* was never finished – near the end of his life, Thomas Aquinas had an experience of God which affected him so powerfully that all his work seemed to him to be like straw.

John Duns Scotus (c.1266–1308), the 'Subtle Doctor' (whose name was later corrupted, rather unfairly, into the word 'Dunce'), developed the thought of Aquinas but argued for a greater freedom in it. His notion was that God did whatever he wanted, rather than making him quite as tightly bound by logical necessity as Aquinas seems to have believed. Duns Scotus's ideas opened up more room for mediaeval scholars to speculate outside the boundaries of Aristotle's logic.

William of Ockham, or Occam, (1287–1347) is best associated with the principle called 'Occam's razor', which was the idea that a more elaborate explanation ought to be ruled out if one with fewer assumptions existed. William was more sceptical about the ability of human logic to explain God and nature, preferring rather the evidence of experience and revelation.

While this is the briefest of introductions to the Scholastics, I hope that it will encourage readers to look into them further, however daunting that may seem. Even Thomas Aquinas's *Summa Theologica*, while long and logical, isn't actually as difficult to read as might be supposed.

GALILEO AND THE BIRTH OF MODERN SCIENCE

Another often quoted example of the church squashing scientific progress is the unfortunate fate of the Italian astronomer Galileo Galilei (1564–1642). In Galileo's time, the Catholic Church came to reject the theory of Nicolaus Copernicus (1473–1543) that the earth moves round the sun – although a person could get round the ban by treating Copernicus's ideas as a model rather than saying that they were true! Galileo, though, used an exceptionally powerful telescope to prove Copernicus right. This was controversial as it seemed to contradict both Scripture and ancient thinkers such as Aristotle and Ptolemy. However, as Galileo himself argued in a letter to a critic, Christine of Lorraine,

Grand Duchess of Tuscany, 'the Holy Spirit's intention is to teach us how to go to heaven, not how the heavens go'.

Nevertheless, Galileo was put on trial as a heretic and convicted. His conviction, however, was largely due to the fact that in his *Dialogue Concerning the Two Chief World Systems* (defending Copernicus) he attributed the words of Pope Urban VIII (initially a supporter of Galileo) to the character Simplicio, thus making him look rather silly. This was unnecessary and unwise. Papal politics therefore played an important role in his eventual condemnation. Yet even though Galileo was found guilty of heresy, he wasn't burned at the stake but rather sentenced to house arrest for the rest of his life.

This whole episode has been rather talked up as proof of an ongoing conflict between religion and science, but it does so in ways that Galileo himself almost certainly never intended (as his own comments about the Holy Spirit's teaching demonstrate). While it is an unpleasant episode in the history of Christianity, it is an overgeneralisation to claim that the fate of Galileo proves that Christianity necessarily holds back scientific advance. It isn't the case that Galileo's achievements somehow came completely out of the blue, following centuries in which reason was drowned out by superstition. I am not in the slightest seeking to downplay what Galileo accomplished. I believe that historian James Hannam gets the balance right when he concludes:

> *Galileo's scientific achievement was solidly based on the natural philosophy that came before him. Appreciating*

> *that fact should not diminish our admiration of his genius. While almost all his theories can be traced back to earlier sources, he was the first to mould them into a coherent whole and the first to show how they could be empirically demonstrated. In that sense, the long road to modern science really does start with him.*[58]

THE BEGINNING OF TIME, AS WE KNOW IT

Many things which advanced human wellbeing, such as the windmill and spectacles, were invented during the Middle Ages. Other technical advances from the East, such as gunpowder and the printing press, were also developed in new ways by mediaeval Christendom. To take one example from this period, the invention of the mechanical clock, which massively shaped the way that we all live today, came about because of Christians.

Historian Daniel J. Boorstin describes the origins of the mechanical clock as follows: 'The first steps towards the mechanical measurement of time, the beginnings of the modern clock in Europe, came not from farmers or shepherds, nor from merchants or craftsmen, but from religious persons anxious to perform promptly and regularly their duties to God. Monks needed to know the times for their appointed prayers.'[59]

In other words, the invention of the mechanical clock began because Christian monks wanted to pray at regular intervals. Yet this regular and accurate measure of the passing hours was also of vital importance for the development of empirical science and significantly changed society, shaping all our days, our work and play, right up to the present time.

AN AGE OF IGNORANCE AND SUPERSTITION?

The developments of mediaeval thinkers (or natural philosophers, as they called themselves) about the natural world thus made a contribution towards laying the foundations of modern science. This was in no small part due to (not despite) their religious faith. Again, James Hannam puts it well: 'Their central belief that nature was created by God and so worthy of their attention was one that Galileo wholeheartedly endorsed. Without that awareness, modern science would simply not have happened.'[60]

For those who might consider this chapter to be Eurocentric – focusing on white men teaching the world how to think – this is not intentionally so. My primary aim here is to counter the idea that mediaeval Europeans barely thought at all! I certainly do not deny the achievements, for instance, of the great mathematicians of India and the Middle East (who gave the world Arabic numerals and the concept of zero, among many other things). Indeed, much of the zeal for learning within later mediaeval Europe seems to have been fuelled by a fear that the West was falling behind other parts of the world in terms of knowledge. People in the Middle Ages built on the achievements of their ancestors, as generations did before them and have done since.

Undoubtedly there were some cases where Christian thinkers came to conclusions that later generations of believers might find embarrassing (though this isn't, of course, only a problem faced by Christians). Nevertheless, in general, scientific and technological advance continued during the mediaeval period. The idea that the coming of Christianity ushered in a new age of ignorance and superstition isn't really borne out by the facts.

SUGGESTED APPLICATIONS

One obvious application for Christians is to be careful about treating the Bible as if it were a scientific textbook, using it to prove things (such as the idea that the sun orbits the earth) which later turn out not to be true. This isn't a new problem. Back in 415 Augustine of Hippo warned, in his *Literal Meaning of Genesis*, that some Christians' interpretations of the Bible risked making Christianity seem absurd and false to educated unbelievers.

At the other end of the scale is the importance of avoiding what the 20th-century Christian author C. S. Lewis called chronological snobbery – the false certainty that we are better and wiser people than those who have gone before us. Much as looking at the scientific mistakes of the past might make us feel intellectually superior, so looking at the barbarity of the Crusades or the Inquisitions might make us feel morally superior to our ancestors. Christians did do terrible things. However, our knowledge springs both from learning from their mistakes and from building upon the foundations which they laid. Furthermore, the atrocities of the 20th and 21st centuries surely should give us pause for thought in assuming our moral progress from our ancestors.

It might be wiser (though much less comfortable) for us to ask instead: what are the great errors and crimes of our age? Are there things which, one day, future generations will look back on, wondering how we could have been so stupid and so cruel?

QUESTIONS FOR FURTHER STUDY

1 Were you taught at school that mediaeval people thought that the world was flat and that early explorers were in danger of falling off the edge?

2 Has this chapter changed your view of the Middle Ages?

3 In your opinion, what are some of the great errors and crimes of our own age?

9

THE PURGING FIRES

About eight miles away from where I live is the town of Lewes in East Sussex. Lewes is famed for its bonfire night celebrations, although some may find the darker undertones of the festivities disturbing, such as the burning of effigies (most notably that of Pope Paul V) and the signs proclaiming 'No popery'. The last time I went, I was with some friends from North America, who were particularly startled by the sight of 17 burning crosses being paraded down the street. I explained that these marked the martyrdoms of 17 Protestants burned at the stake in Lewes during the reign of Queen Mary (1555–1558). This was a time when men and women would die and kill for the faith.

This troubled period can be characterised by two sets of fires. The first was the widely held belief (in the West at least) of the purging fire, or purgatory, which would cleanse believers after death. The second was the discontent and rebellion against religious authority which reached its climax in the Protestant Reformation of the early 16th century. This, in turn, was often responded to by the church authorities with literal fire – the burning of heretics at the stake.

THE FIRES OF PURGATORY

According to traditional Catholic theology, the fire of purgatory purifies those who die in a state of grace before they enter heaven. Purgatory was an important concern in the later Middle Ages, as was the buying and selling of indulgences to enable yourself, or someone else, to get through it reasonably unsinged. In fact, it was these indulgences which sparked the Protestant Reformation in the first place.

Over the centuries a few scriptural passages have been used to defend this doctrine of purgatory. Matthew 12:32, for instance, says, 'Anyone who speaks a word against the Son of Man will be forgiven, but anyone who speaks against the Holy Spirit will not be forgiven, either in this age or in the age to come.' This is taken to imply (however indirectly) that some sins might be forgiven in the age to come. Likewise, the references in Matthew 5:25–26 to a prison, where you might ultimately be thrown, and in Philippians 2:10 to a place 'under the earth', where people bow the knee to Jesus, have been understood as referring to purgatory. More controversially, appeal has been made to the apocryphal 2 Maccabees 12:40–44, where prayers and a collection of money are offered to God to atone for the sins of some Jewish soldiers who had died with idolatrous tokens hidden under their clothes. The main case for purgatory, however, has been 1 Corinthians 3:10-15, where Paul writes:

> *By the grace God has given me, I laid a foundation as a wise builder, and someone else is building on it. But each one should build with care. For no one can lay any foundation other than the one already laid, which is Jesus Christ. If anyone builds on this foundation using gold, silver, costly stones, wood, hay or straw, their work will be shown for what it is, because the Day will bring it to light. It will be revealed with fire, and the fire will test the quality of each person's work. If what has been built survives, the builder will receive a reward. If it is burned up, the builder will suffer loss but yet will be saved – even though only as one escaping through the flames.*

Back in the early church, Augustine of Hippo had interpreted this passage as referring to the one who, although saved, feels the loss of worldly attachments, and who:

> *... prefers the alternative of going without these things to going without Christ and does not forsake Christ out of fear of losing them – though he grieve ever so much in losing them – he is saved, yet so as by fire, for he burns with grief over the things he has lost; but it does not overwhelm or consume him, fortified as he is by the firmness and the indestructability of his foundation.*

> *That something similar may take place after this life is not impossible. The question whether such is the case, is justified and may yield to a solution or remain in doubt: the question whether some of the faithful are saved by a sort of purgatorial fire, and this later or sooner according as they have loved more or less the goods that perish.*[61]

As we can see, Augustine understands purgatory here as the pain of losing things to which you had been attached, and which were considered as wood, hay or straw compared with the gold, silver and costly stones of Christ. His focus is on loss in this life, but he does suggest that this suffering might also continue for a while after death.

This idea came to be understood as indicating the need for cleansing for those who, while saved, had not yet attained sufficient holiness in their lives to enter and enjoy heaven. Here lies the root of the problem. If heaven is only for perfect people, then surely imperfect people couldn't be let in. But if these imperfect people were genuine believers, it also seemed wrong to suggest that they would be condemned to hell. The Venerable Bede (673–735) is among those who preached in this way. On the basis of the existence of purgatory, he argued that even serious sinners who repented on their death beds could (eventually) get into heaven.

During the 13th century (most notably at the Second Council of Lyons in 1274) purgatory was confirmed in the West as a definite teaching, which all Christians were expected to believe. As the Middle Ages progressed, the idea also developed to include the possibility that people could buy indulgences from the pope (or his salesmen) to get themselves, or their deceased relatives and friends, out of purgatory (or at least to lessen their sufferings). This development came from the idea that the pope had a 'treasury of merits' formed by those saints who did more meritorious works than they needed to do. It was thought that these spare 'merits' could instead be used to help dead believers in purgatory. Therefore, indulgences were initially offered by the pope to those who went on crusade, or who completed some other significant work of penance. Eventually, though, a cash payment was deemed enough for someone to be granted an indulgence.

According to C. S. Lewis (himself a believer in the earlier idea of purgatory as a final cleansing) the Protestant Reformers had good reason for their doubts about purgatory.[62] Not only was there the scandal of the sale of indulgences, but the doctrine itself had become degraded. Dante's Purgatorio in the 13th century had portrayed purgatory as a place of painful cleansing. Thomas More's Supplication of Souls in the 16th century, by contrast, seemed to portray it as a place of retribution, where the sufferings of the deceased made them forget God rather than draw near to him, as though God were somehow getting even.

So what had started out as an idea that a saved person might need to let go of their remaining worldly attachments before entering heaven had ended up as something more akin to a divine hostage situation, with people being asked for money to pay for God to release their dead relatives from torture![63]

THE FIRES OF DISCONTENT

Dissatisfaction with the state of the mediaeval Catholic Church, such as with this practice of buying indulgences, was clear to see in the Protestant Reformation. Yet rumblings of discontent could be heard already in the Middle Ages, and these helped pave the way for later, more radical, reform.

Problems for the popes

The idea that the Bishop of Rome was pre-eminent among the bishops of the church was already fairly well established in the early centuries of Christianity. What was disputed by the East (and came to be disputed even more in the West at the Reformation) was the pope's claim to leadership over all churches, as Christ's representative on earth and as the successor of Peter, the head of the apostles.

In addition, the pope had come to claim political as well as spiritual authority. Some of these political assertions rested on a document known as the *Donation of Constantine*. This maintained that Emperor Constantine had granted political authority to the pope over all of Western Europe when he moved his capital from Rome to Constantinople (modern Istanbul).

In 1440, the scholar Lorenzo Vallo published his discovery that this document was actually an eighth-century forgery, thus threatening the pope's authority. This authority, however, had already been under threat. During the 14th century, a series of French popes had ruled from Avignon in southern France. This resulted in a revolt in Italy, from where popes more traditionally came, and the election of a rival, Italian pope.

This new Great Schism[64] was then deepened by an unsuccessful attempt at Pisa in 1409 to depose both existing popes in favour of a third claimant. Instead of replacing two popes with one, this solution made the problem worse by resulting in three popes, all claiming to be Christ's representative on earth! Eventually, the Council of Constance (1414–1418) resolved the issue by agreeing on a single pope to replace all the existing incumbents. Even then, though, there were still some die-hard supporters of the pope in Avignon, who hadn't understood the message of unity. This confusing situation lasted for nearly half a century and split the allegiances of European rulers, raising all sorts of awkward questions about who the real pope was.

Another result of this schism was the rise of Conciliarism, a movement within the Catholic Church which argued that supreme authority didn't rest with the pope but with a council of the whole church – as the East believed. As it was a council which had ended the schism and elected a new pope to replace the previous three, this was taken as proof that the council had more authority than the pope. This attempted move away from papal rule was doggedly resisted by the papacy, although it wasn't until 1870 that it asserted papal infallibility[65] as a church dogma.

Reform movements

However, even before the papacy had suffered these blows to its reputation, dissent had already begun to grow within Europe about the perceived corruption of the church.

The Lollards (literally 'mumblers') were a reform movement which arose in 14th- and 15th-century England, a time marked by devastating plague, social unrest and a war between the English and the French which lingered, on and off, for more than a century. The Lollards followed the teachings of John Wycliffe (c. 1320s–1384), who criticised the authority of the pope, the wealth and hierarchy of the church and even the doctrine of transubstantiation concerning the Lord's Supper.[66] Wycliffe's disciples also produced a translation of the Bible in Middle English, although this was from the Latin version rather than from the original Hebrew and Greek.

Wycliffe avoided persecution as a result of being protected by King Edward III's son, Edward the Black Prince, who was supportive of Lollard ideas. Nevertheless, Wycliffe was still condemned as a heretic after his death in 1415 and his body burned.

Another leading critic from this time was Jan Hus (c. 1369–1415), a Czech priest and a famous preacher in Prague, who criticised abuses in the church. He insisted in particular on communion 'in both kinds', whereby people received both bread and wine in communion, rather than just the bread alone as was the practice in the West at the time.[67] He also insisted that worship should be conducted in the people's native language rather than in Latin.

Hus was excommunicated in 1411 and summoned to the Council of Constance in 1415 with guarantees of safe conduct. However, these guarantees proved not worth the paper they were written on, and were soon discarded on the grounds that promises made to a heretic weren't binding. Hus was burned at the stake following several months of imprisonment.

Before his death, Hus is alleged to have made a prophecy in prison that although the church was going to burn a 'goose' (the meaning of his name), within a hundred years they would hear a swan sing which they would not be able to silence. Martin Luther, who went on to lead the Protestant Reformation a century later, applied this prophecy to himself.

Erasmus, Tyndale and the New Testament

Another critic (who nevertheless remained within the Catholic Church) was the writer Desiderius Erasmus of Rotterdam (1466–1536). Erasmus's greatest contribution to the growing reform movement was his production, in 1516, of a printed edition of the New Testament in the original Greek, with a parallel Latin text. This corrected the official Latin translation, the Vulgate, and was soon being used to produce translations of the New Testament in various European languages, enabling ordinary people to read them.

In 1526, the Englishman William Tyndale produced, in exile, the first translation of the New Testament into English directly from the Greek. However, his work was condemned back home by the Lord Chancellor, Sir Thomas More, as a false translation on the grounds that it 'mistranslated' several key words, including:

agapē	translated as 'love' rather than 'charity'
homologeō	translated as 'acknowledge' rather than 'confess'
metanoia	translated as 'repentance' rather than 'penance'
presbyteros	translated as 'senior' (1526) or 'elder' (1534) rather than 'priest'
ekklēsia	translated as 'congregation' rather than 'church'

While Tyndale's translations were true to the meanings of the Greek words, they were controversial because they appeared to undermine the mediaeval Catholic interpretations of those words. The irony was that Tyndale's interpretations of some of these Greek words wasn't much different from Erasmus's, whom Thomas More considered a good friend.

Tyndale paid for his translation work with his life. He was strangled and burned at the stake outside Brussels in 1536. Nevertheless, his revised edition of the New

Testament was highly influential on subsequent English translations. Indeed, the New Testament text of the King James Bible of 1611 is about two-thirds identical to Tyndale's second edition of 1634. Even many modern translations are indebted to his pioneering work. Thus while Tyndale's voice of protest had been silenced by fire, it was much too late from the authorities' point of view. By then an even bigger fire had already broken out across much of central Europe, a fire which would purge Western Christianity and which is, to a large degree, still alight.

SUGGESTED APPLICATION

What stands out from this age is the importance placed on people reading the Scriptures. Giving individuals the ability to read the Bible in their own language had been a key demand of reformers. Some of those who were burned at Lewes died for 'crimes' no more serious than reading the Bible in English, or allowing others to read it. Perhaps the main application that we can take from this period is to be grateful that we can read the Scriptures for ourselves and to allow those Scriptures, God's words to us, to shape our lives.

QUESTIONS FOR FURTHER STUDY

1 Before reading this chapter, what was your opinion of purgatory? Has that opinion changed? Which (if any) of the different views of purgatory could you support? Can you think of any other passages of Scripture to support or reject these ideas?

2 What do you think is the best way for the church to respond to criticism? Do you think that we currently react well to being criticised?

3 If we have any criticism or correction to bring to others, what is the best way to do it?

4 How can we better allow the Scriptures, God's words to us, to shape our lives?

10

REFORM AND RADICALISM

Unless I am convinced by the testimony of Holy Scripture or by evident reason – for I can believe neither popes nor councils alone, as it is evident that they have erred repeatedly and contradicted themselves – my conscience is bound to the Word of God. Thus I cannot and will not recant, because acting against conscience is neither safe nor sound. Here I stand. I can do no other. God help me.[68]

It was with these words (or words very much like them) that a German monk and theologian took a stand against the entire mediaeval church establishment. He refused to disown his writings, even though they had been condemned by the Catholic Church. Instead, he acted on the basis of his own conscience and his understanding of what the Bible clearly taught. His name was Martin Luther and his defiance started a revolution within Christianity, one which endures to this day – and which probably went a good deal further than he himself intended.

MARTIN LUTHER AND THE REFORMATION

In his early days, though, Martin Luther (1483–1546) was an unlikely reformer. He had been a law student in Erfurt, in what is now Germany. Yet one day, when caught outside in a lightning storm, he made a vow to St Anne that he would become a monk if he lived. His life was spared, so he duly became first an Augustinian monk and then a priest. But even then he made an inauspicious start when, during his first mass, he was apparently so struck with awe at the holiness and majesty of God that he struggled to complete the service. Initially he also was very much a participant in the Catholic Church's practices, making a pilgrimage to Rome to say mass for his dead mother and to climb the Holy Stairs on his knees on behalf of his dead grandfather. Nevertheless, he was troubled by doubts as to whether these acts had done any good for their souls in purgatory.

It was during his time as a doctor of theology at Wittenberg that the crisis erupted which was to trigger the Reformation. A travelling preacher named Johann Tetzel (1464–1519) arrived in town, selling indulgences from the pope. As we saw in the last chapter, it was said that these indulgences could rescue people's loved ones and themselves from the fires of purgatory. Tetzel's sales pitch included the following catchy slogan:

Wenn das Geld in Kasten klingt,
Die Seele aus dem Feuer springt!

When the money rings in the casket,
The soul springs out of the fire [of purgatory].

Luther, concerned by this theology and practice of selling indulgences, was spurred into action. He responded on 31 October 1517 by issuing his famous 95 theses (or points for discussion), demanding that a formal debate take place about indulgences. One of the most stinging attacks in this document went as follows:

(82) Why does not the Pope empty purgatory on account of most holy charity and the great need of souls, the most righteous of causes, seeing that he redeems an infinite number of souls on account of sordid money, given for the erection of a basilica, which is a most trivial cause?

In other words, Luther was asking that if the pope truly has the keys to the 'treasury of merits' and can release souls from the pains of purgatory, then why do people need to pay him money? Why doesn't he just issue indulgences for free? One reason may well have been that the pope needed to raise enough money to build St Peter's Basilica in Rome.

The 95 theses had originally been written in Latin, the language of academic debate. Soon, however, Luther would take the bold step of publishing his ideas in German, the language of the ordinary people. With the help of the new technology of the printing press, Luther's criticisms of the Catholic Church and her practices quickly spread far and wide.

The following April, Luther took part in a public debate (now known as the Heidelberg Disputation) with his fellow monks on these issues. Later that year he was summoned to appear before Cardinal Cajetan and ordered to recant his views but refused to do so. Matters came to a head in 1520 when Martin Luther was excommunicated from the Catholic Church on the grounds that he attacked papal authority; spread false opinions about the sacraments, purgatory and confession (Luther believed that ordinary people could hear confessions as well as priests); and taught that the burning of heretics grieved the Holy Spirit.

In 1521, Luther was summoned before the Diet of Worms (an imperial council in the German town of Worms), where he again refused to recant, arguing – as we have already seen – that his conscience was bound to the Word of God. Luther would have known what had happened to the Czech reformer Jan Hus, a century before, and must have suspected that he was probably going to his death. Nevertheless, he still went and stood up for what he believed to be true, whatever the cost to himself.

As it turned out, the council did indeed condemn him as a heretic and declared him an outlaw. However, Luther had powerful friends to protect him, most notably Frederick III, Prince-Elector of Saxony. They staged an abduction to capture Luther and hide him away at Frederick's castle in

Wartburg, where he would be safe. Luther spent his time at Wartburg in producing a translation of the Bible in German so that ordinary Germans could study Scripture for themselves.

Luther's theological revolution

Luther's biggest contribution to Christian doctrine was his understanding of what is called 'justification through faith alone'. According to this teaching, sinful people can be declared righteous by God and receive all that Christ achieved on their behalf simply through putting their trust in him. It was (and is) a radical idea. It liberated Luther from years of trying to save himself and he couldn't keep quiet about it for the sake of others.

'Justification through faith alone' became the watchword of the Reformation and the teaching which most set Protestants (as they became known) apart from Catholics. Oddly enough, one of the best accounts that I have found on this subject comes from a Catholic author, Peter Kreeft, who writes:

> *Luther's story is well known. Passionate, impetuous, demanding, sensitive, and pessimistic in temperament, Luther had never been able to find inner peace. He could not overcome his sense of guilt despite all his good works, prayers, penances and alms. His confessor advised him to read Romans. No more historically momentous advice was ever given by a confessor. In Romans Luther discovered the simple bombshell truth that God had forgiven his sins*

> *freely, not because of Luther's works in Germany but because of Christ's work on Calvary. That discovery freed Luther's spirit and ignited a fire that swept over Europe.*[69]

So what about good works then? If these are no longer seen to be the means of our salvation, are they to be discarded? Not at all! For Luther, justification through faith didn't mean rejecting good works. Rather faith enables and empowers them. Christians are meant to do good works out of love to others and gratitude for God's mercy, not as a way of trying to earn God's favour. 'And this …' as Peter Kreeft goes on to say, 'is winsome. No one wants to be loved as someone else's good deed for the day.'

The distinctive theological views of Luther and his followers were proclaimed in the Augsburg Confession of 1530. This confession of faith (a common practice among early Protestants) is still a key text of Lutheranism. Yet, while it strongly emphasises justification through faith alone, it would surprise many people to know that it is still a lot closer in much of its theology to the Catholic Church than most other branches of Protestantism. For example, many Lutherans still believe in baptismal regeneration;[70] the real and physical presence of the body and blood of Christ in the Lord's Supper; confession and absolution; liturgical worship; and some use of images in church.

A flawed hero

Martin Luther, while to many the hero of the Reformation, was nonetheless a man of many weaknesses. He is recorded as having had a foul temper and often used coarse and abusive language. While he had defended Jews against prejudice in the early days of the Reformation, he hardened in his attitudes as time went on and towards the end of his life, it is sad to say, he became particularly anti-Semitic. Nevertheless, he should still be remembered as a courageous man who risked his life in order to reform abuses within the church.

It is also worth recording the fact that Lutheran theologians conducted a respectful and friendly dialogue (in Greek) with the Patriarch of Constantinople between 1559 and 1581, though they were ultimately unable to fulfil their desire to reunite with the Orthodox Christians in the East.

THE REFORMATION BECOMES RADICAL

Like Luther, Huldrych (or Ulrich) Zwingli (1484–1531) – a priest and scholar from Zurich and effective leader of the Swiss Reformation – believed in using Scripture as the primary source of his beliefs. Yet this resulted in Zwingli coming to far more radical conclusions than Luther had. Zwingli always insisted that he came to his theological opinions directly from Scripture and independently of Martin Luther and events in Germany. He was also fluent in Greek and read widely the writings of early church fathers. Unusually for a church pastor, though, he died in battle.

Zwingli came to understand the sacraments of baptism and the Lord's Supper mainly as memorials (or symbols) rather than as means of receiving God's grace, although he still believed in baptising infants. He came to oppose church disciplines such as Lent, although he believed in fasting in private. He came to oppose church government by bishops and the traditional understanding of the priesthood, although this (unfortunately) resulted in a greater role for the state in matters of church discipline and government. He was critical of the lax sexual morals among the clergy of his time, arguing in favour of a married priesthood, although his own personal life in this area was itself not entirely beyond reproach. Like many other reformers, he opposed prayers to Mary and the saints, as well as prayers for the dead. In many ways, it is Zwingli rather than Luther who established the doctrines familiar to most evangelicals.

However, the Reformation soon became far more radical than even Zwingli had anticipated. The Anabaptists under Thomas Müntzer (1489–1525) – the leader of a peasants' revolt in Germany – and Balthasar Hubmeier (1480–1528) – one of the leading theologians of Anabaptism – came to reject infant baptism and any role for the state in church affairs. Some Anabaptists were alleged to have advocated both anarchy and Communism.

Both Luther and Zwingli were fearful of what they saw as the dire social and religious consequences of this lawlessness and anarchy. They therefore lent their support to the authorities' use of violence to bring the dissidents back in line. The peasants' revolt in Germany was violently crushed by the princes with Luther's support. Likewise, in Switzerland, Zwingli acquiesced in the decision that Anabaptist leaders be drowned in mockery of their practice of baptising adult believers by full immersion.

Soon, though, a synthesis between the relative conservatism of Luther and the radicalism of Zwingli was to be found in the theology of a French lawyer and exile in Geneva, John Calvin (as we shall see in the next chapter).

SUGGESTED APPLICATIONS

One of the lessons to be learnt from this period is avoiding the sort of religious hucksterism characterised by Johann Tetzel's sale of indulgences. It is sadly still too easy for Christians to get caught up in this sort of thing. Without wanting to be judgemental, some modern 'prosperity theology' doesn't seem to me to be a million miles away from Tetzel's approach.

There are also lessons here when it comes to applying Christian teaching on faith and works. At one extreme we can fall into the trap of trying to earn our way into heaven. At the other extreme it is possible to forget that faith in Christ is meant to lead us into a life of love for God and others, full of good works.

A final lesson is that it is much easier to start a revolution then it is to stop it again. Zwingli took things much further than Luther ever intended. The Anabaptists, in turn, took things much further than Zwingli ever intended. Both Luther and Zwingli were aghast at the outcome.

QUESTIONS FOR FURTHER STUDY

1 Can you think of any other examples where a reform movement has become more radical than was intended by those who started it? This isn't necessarily limited to religious reform.

2 How can we avoid religious hucksterism? What do we mean by this? Can it happen today?

3 Do you try to earn God's favour?

4 What good works are there in your life as a result of your faith in Christ?

11

FIGHTING OVER FAITH

Catholics, Orthodox, Copts, Lutherans, Anglicans, Presbyterians, Congregationalists, Baptists, Quakers: the list goes on and on. In the New Testament there was only one Christian church, so where did all these denominations come from?

While some splits (such as that between the Catholics and the Copts, or between Catholics and the Eastern Orthodox Church) took place in earlier centuries, the seeds of denominational Christianity were sown at the Reformation and in the divisions which followed. The Reformation and the Catholic Church's response to it resulted in wars of religion. Protestants also continued to divide themselves into different groups. Much of this fighting over faith was literal combat – a bloody war which tore Europe apart. Other fighting was less bloody – a war of words and ideas with competing understandings of theology.[71]

THE COUNTER-REFORMATION

The Counter-Reformation was the Catholic fight back against the religious revolution which Luther and Zwingli had unleashed. This is sometimes called the Catholic Reformation since it addressed some of the abuses – such as the sale of indulgences – which had provoked the Reformation in the first place.

Initially this counterattack was unsuccessful as a string of short-lived popes proved unable to implement the reforms which critics of the church had been seeking for generations. Eventually, however, one reforming pope, John III (who reigned from 1534 to 1549), made three key decisions which finally enabled the Catholic Church to regain much of its control in Europe and beyond:

1. The establishment of the Jesuit Order in 1540, under Ignatius Loyola. This significantly improved Catholic educational structures. It also engaged in missionary activity, both in Protestant areas of Europe and beyond (especially in the Far East and in Latin America).
2. The establishment of a Roman Inquisition with a mandate to stamp out Protestantism.
3. The calling of the Council of Trent (1545–1563), which clarified Catholic teaching, especially regarding the disputed issues of justification and the sacraments. It also reformed abuses such as the sale of indulgences and pronounced anathemas

> (or curses) on Protestants and, to a more limited extent, on the Eastern Orthodox Church as well.

The battle between the Reformation and the Counter-Reformation led to generations of war in Western Europe. The most notorious of these was the brutal Thirty Years' War (1618–1648), which decimated large parts of Germany. By the end of it the Catholic Church had succeeded in drastically reducing the number of states and territories in Europe under Protestant rule or cultural dominance. The fight back was under way.

CALVINISM

During this period, however, a third champion of the Protestant Reformation arose: John Calvin. He steered a path between Luther's more conservative aims and the radicalism of Zwingli and others, and his influence extends widely throughout Protestantism today (even among those who reject his theology).

John Calvin (1509–1564) was born in Noyon in France and studied in Paris. He had originally intended to study for the priesthood and managed to attain a competence in both Hebrew and Greek in addition to fluency in Latin and his native French. Yet while at Paris he gave up his ambition to become a priest and trained instead as a lawyer.

During his 20s Calvin underwent a dramatic conversion to Protestantism. In 1535, after religious tensions had resulted in widespread violence against Protestant Christians in France, Calvin fled to Switzerland to avoid the unpleasant possibility of being burned at the stake as a heretic. The following year, while staying overnight in Geneva, he was accosted by a Swiss reformer, Guillaume Farel (1489–1565), who implored him to remain and undertake the reformation of the city. Calvin remained as the leader of this Reformed Church of Geneva until his death, despite early setbacks, including a time when he was forced to flee the town, resulting in him spending several years in Strasbourg.

Calvin's theology stood firmly between the conservatives and the radicals. For example, when it came to understanding the Lord's Supper, Calvin held (against the radicals) that Christ was really present at the Supper, but also argued (against the Catholics and Lutherans) that the bread and wine didn't physically become or contain Christ's body and blood. Calvin believed in the baptism of infants (unlike the Anabaptists) but he didn't believe that baptism caused those infants to be born again (unlike Catholics and Lutherans). Calvin didn't want rule by bishops but he still believed that church discipline should be used against those who didn't live out their profession of faith in practice.

Calvin's greatest work is the *Institutes of the Christian Religion* (the final version of which was published in 1556). This is divided into four books, focusing on God, humanity, salvation and the church. Calvin didn't merely express a few opinions on the disputes of his time. Instead, he created a systematic theology, which drew upon Scripture and the writings of earlier Christian thinkers, most notably Augustine of Hippo. Calvin wasn't afraid to take on difficult subjects or come to unpopular conclusions. The intellectual appeal of Calvinism as a doctrinal system, in which people can engage their minds, is surely one reason why his theology remains so widely held today.

Another possible reason for the enduring popularity of Calvinism is Calvin's high view of divine sovereignty. Many have drawn great comfort from the belief that God is completely in charge of the world, even when things seem to be going badly wrong, and from Calvin's teaching that God specifically chose people to come to faith. According to Calvin, if you are a believer, this means that God individually loved you and chose you even before the world began.

However, it is also true to say that Calvin's high view of God's control over the world does raise some difficult questions. For example, Calvin went as far as to say that evil acts cannot happen unless God, in some sense, wills them to happen. He believed that before the world began God not only predestined those who were going to be saved but also those who were to be damned – a view known as double predestination. More controversially still, Calvin taught a 'temporary faith of the reprobate' whereby God sometimes gives a taste of grace and faith to those whom he does not intend to finally save. Calvin used this to explain the phenomenon of those who seem to believe for a while but then turn away from faith. Ultimately, however, it led to pastoral difficulties since it could severely undermine believers' assurance of their own salvation. After all, how can someone know that their own faith isn't temporary? Calvin accepted that these ideas were 'horrible'[72] but still maintained them to be true. Today, though, many Calvinists have much more moderate views on these questions.

Other issues Calvin faced were similar to those encountered by different Protestant reformers. One such problem (as we also saw in the last chapter) was that breaking away from the pope's control of the church opened the door to the state controlling the church. In Geneva, this resulted in continuing harsh punishments for offenders, including heretics.[73]

John Calvin's model of church government in Geneva laid the foundations for Presbyterian and Reformed churches across Europe, North America and beyond. The Reformation of the Church of Scotland under John Knox (1513–1572) was heavily influenced by Calvin's model, and his theology was also held, and developed, in England (and in New England) by the Puritans.

REFORMED CHALLENGES TO CALVINISM

As already seen, Calvin held some controversial views. These did not go unquestioned, even by those who were broadly sympathetic to his wider aims, resulting in a couple of potential challengers.

Challenger number one: Arminius

In 1603, James Arminius (1560–1609), a minister in the Reformed Church in the Netherlands,[74] began openly questioning the Calvinist understanding of predestination.

Arminius's main concern appears to have been that this teaching could seem to make God the author of evil. It also seemed to portray him as making an offer of salvation to people whom he had already decided couldn't even want to receive it.

Arminius argued that instead of predestining specific individuals to belief or unbelief, God had achieved through Christ's life, death and resurrection the possibility of salvation for everybody, and had predestined to salvation everyone who believes in Christ. God naturally knows from eternity who will and who won't believe. This teaching sought to ensure that the responsibility for damnation is placed firmly on the unbeliever, while still asserting that salvation comes from God.

Arminius's teaching was criticised on the ground that it gave too much credit to the believer in their own salvation. However, Arminius, no less than Calvin, believed that fallen human beings were utterly unable even to want to receive Christ unless divine grace enabled them to do so, or to remain believers unless divine grace helped them. Unlike Calvin, though, Arminius held that this grace was potentially available to everyone, enabling them either to accept or to reject the offer of salvation in the gospel.

Calvinism responds: the five petals of the tulip

In 1619, the opinions of Arminius's followers (known as the Remonstrants) were rejected by the Synod of Dort, a church council in the Netherlands. Since the Remonstrants had set out their arguments in five points, the Calvinists came up with five points of their own. These 'five points of Calvinism' were later summarised with the acronym TULIP:

- **T** is for **total depravity**: every area of our lives is affected by sin, making us unable to even want to be saved without God's grace.
- **U** is for **unconditional election**: God chooses who will be saved on the basis of his own good pleasure and not because of anything in us.
- **L** is for **limited atonement**: Christ died on behalf of those whom he had chosen for salvation and not for everyone in the world.[75]
- **I** is for **irresistible grace**: God draws irresistibly those whom he has chosen for salvation, so that they do not even want to resist him.
- **P** is for **perseverance of the saints**: those whom God has chosen for salvation can never fully nor finally fall away from the faith – even though they still sin; God will surely preserve them so that they persevere in faith and repentance until the end of their lives and are saved. The later teaching 'once saved, always saved' is a development of this point.

Challenger number two: Amyraut

Moise Amyraut, also known as Moses Amyraldus (1596–1664), developed another modification of Calvinism. This is known as Amyraldism or 'four-point Calvinism', and is still with us today.

Amyraut argued that Christ achieved salvation on the cross for everybody in the world and that anybody can receive this salvation by faith. However, he coupled this universal offer with a more traditionally Calvinist view of predestination in which the faith needed to receive salvation is granted only to those whom God has chosen before the beginning of the world. His system, therefore, is a hypothetical universalism which turns out to be quite Calvinistic in practice. Whatever one thinks of his scheme, Amyraut should be commended for his willingness to defend his opponents when he thought that their positions were being misrepresented by his own supporters.

A MIDDLE WAY BETWEEN ROME AND GENEVA?

The Reformation in England and Wales and its fluctuating success was closely bound up with the family history of the Tudors. Henry VIII, who reigned from 1509 up to his death in 1547, broke away from Rome, dissolved the monasteries and made himself Supreme Head of the Church of England, while remaining otherwise essentially Catholic in terms of his theology. His son, Edward VI, was a more thorough Protestant and reformed the church in a Calvinistic direction, but he was a child when he became king and reigned only six years (1547–1553). Henry's eldest daughter, Mary I, in her five-year rule (1553–1558), tried to reverse the Reformation and restore the Catholic Church, in the process burning around 300 Protestants at the stake.

Finally, Elizabeth I, Henry's second daughter, who ruled from 1558 to 1603, adopted the slightly less exalted title of Supreme Governor of the Church of England and opted, in the interests of peace, for a *via media* ('middle way') between Rome and Geneva. This was a type of Reformed Catholicism, drawn up (rather ambiguously) in the '39 Articles of Religion' (1571).

This middle way had some success in containing the wars of religion. In England and Wales, at least, the slaughter was less than in much of the rest of Europe. Even so, this compromise couldn't prevent religious differences from becoming an issue in the civil wars which broke out in the 17th century.

RELIGION AND REVOLUTION IN 17TH-CENTURY BRITAIN AND IRELAND

In 1603, James VI of Scotland became James I of England, thus uniting the crowns of England (at that time including Wales), Scotland and Ireland, though there were still separate parliaments and governments for each of the three realms. A key development of this period was James I's commissioning of the King James Bible of 1611, which largely replaced the Geneva Bible[76] and other earlier English translations.

James' reign promised both a stable Protestant succession and greater toleration for Catholics. However, the pledged toleration didn't materialise. The Gunpowder Plot of 5 November 1605 – a failed Catholic assassination attempt on James I and his Parliament – ended hopes that

Catholics could legally co-exist with Protestants, a situation not resolved until Catholic Emancipation in 1829.

Protestant histories of this period often overlook the experience of the Catholic population and portray them as the 'bad guys'. Certainly the fate of the Protestant martyrs should not be ignored. However, it should also be borne in mind that Catholics in Britain during this time had no legal right to practise their religion, hold public office or go to university, and were at risk of fines and the confiscation of their property. During the reigns of Elizabeth and James, Catholic priests were not infrequently put to death as traitors by being publicly hung up, castrated and disembowelled alive! Perhaps it is therefore better to see this period of history as a time of mutual hostility between professing Christians, rather than in the simplistic terms of the 'bad guys' on 'their' side persecuting the 'good guys' on 'our' side of the dispute.

James I and his son Charles I, who became king in 1625, also took issue with the Puritans (the 'hotter sort of Protestants'), as Elizabeth I had done before them. The Puritans wanted a more thoroughly reformed church than the Anglican compromise which had been reached under Elizabeth. During Charles I's reign, this opposition increased as Archbishop William Laud sought to restore a more ornate and liturgical form of worship under the motto 'The beauty of holiness' (taken from the wording of Psalm 29:2 in the King James Bible).

The various political and religious disputes between Charles and his Puritan-dominated Parliament ultimately led to 11 years when the king ruled alone, without a Parliament. They were followed by the English Civil War, the execution of the king in 1649 and the establishment of a Commonwealth (or Republic) which lasted until 1660. The Civil War saw fighting all across the British and Irish isles, with particular brutality being used to subdue Ireland.

One of the most important developments within this period was the rise of dissenting Protestant groups – Presbyterians, Congregationalists, Baptists, Quakers and other independent or 'gathered' churches. Many of these groups were quite radical. The Quakers, in particular, were notable for their focus on the 'inner light' of God rather than outward religious trappings, as well as being very egalitarian, with both men and women serving as ministers. The suppression of the Anglican establishment during the Republic enabled these groups to grow and flourish to the extent that even a crackdown on dissenting views following King Charles II's return was unable to destroy them.

Another key advance took place in religious freedom within Britain at this time. In 1655, Oliver Cromwell, as Lord Protector, allowed the return of Jews to Britain after roughly four centuries of expulsion. However, while Cromwell's commitment to religious toleration was greater than that of many of his contemporaries, it didn't extend to Catholics or even to convinced Anglicans.

SUGGESTED APPLICATION

This was an eventful period, full of professing Christians

opposing and even persecuting one another. While (I am glad to say) most of the mutual hatred has faded away, many of the divisions between Christians which came into being at this time still continue. In the light of them, one obvious application is to consider the importance of fairly understanding and representing other points of view, particularly those which challenge our own deeply held convictions. How well do you cope when your theological beliefs are opposed by other believers? Do you seek to understand what it is that they are really trying to say, or do you rush in to defend your views or attack your opponents? How quick are you to doubt the salvation of Christians from other 'tribes' or to label them as heretics?

None of this is seeking to downplay the importance of right doctrine. I am very far from arguing for a watered-down, dogma-light, lowest-common-denominator Christianity of ethics rather than beliefs. Not all doctrines, though, are of equal importance and they are not all equally clear (especially such issues as the eternal decrees of divine predestination). Rather it is because of the *importance* of Christian doctrine that it is right for us to be sure what we understand – we ought to be wary of making assumptions which may not be true. Sometimes a little humility can go a long way.

QUESTIONS FOR FURTHER STUDY

1 Can you think of any ways in which you could help promote greater unity among Christians? Do you think that this is a good thing?

2 How do you understand the relationship between God's sovereignty and human responsibility and freedom?

3 How well do you cope when your theological beliefs are opposed or questioned? Do you fight back? Do you seek to understand your opponent's point of view? Have you ever tried to defend an opponent who was being misrepresented?

4 In your view, how much of the conflict in this period was caused by genuine religious differences and how much of it by political or other social factors?

12

WAKE UP BRITAIN!

As I mentioned in the introduction, I once participated in some street theatre as part of the Brighton Festival. I played the part of George Whitefield, a widely travelled preacher and evangelist from the 18th century, who preached the good news of Jesus Christ to hundreds of thousands of people across Great Britain and along the eastern seaboard of North America. An astonishing number responded to the gospel.

In fact Whitefield was only one of a number of itinerant preachers from this time who brought the good news to people where they were, at some personal cost.[77] This evangelistic revival had profound effects on Great Britain and beyond and became known as the Great Awakening.

RELIGION AND THE RESTORATION OF THE MONARCHY

In 1660, the Puritan-dominated republican regime came to an end with the return of the 'merry monarch' Charles

II, who reigned until 1685. While Charles himself was a tolerant man and relatively indifferent to matters of religion (although he did convert to Catholicism on his death bed), the same cannot be said for all his ministers. Some of them were eager to restore the Church of England to its former position of authority and to crack down on the Puritans and others whom they blamed for the fate of Charles I. Therefore, shortly on the heels of the restoration of the monarchy came renewed persecution of religious dissenters (although for Catholics such discrimination had never really gone away).

Under the 1662 Clarendon Code (named after Lord Clarendon, one of Charles II's leading ministers) Anglicanism was restored as the established church; dissenting pastors were forced out of the church; private religious gatherings were restricted; and dissenting congregations were menaced, sometimes by gangs of ruffians.

The situation changed in 1689, following the Glorious Revolution of 1688. Through this the Catholic James II was overthrown in favour of his daughter, Mary II, and her husband, William III. Dissenters or non-conformist Protestants were now granted legal toleration although even then Anglicanism still enjoyed a privileged status.

Yet generations of religious strife appear to have taken their toll on the population and the later 17th and earlier 18th centuries were a period of decline in religious certainty. The growing rationalism of the age led to the idea of Deism, in which God was largely reduced to the concept of a watchmaker who wound up the universe and left it to carry on by itself, without much active involvement. (However, it continued to be widely believed that God still rewarded the good and punished the evil after death.) Furthermore, the beginnings of the industrial revolution removed a growing number of people from their traditional rural settings to overcrowded cities. As the organisation of the church (especially the system of local parishes) did not keep up with these demographic changes, the church became increasingly less relevant to people's day-to-day lives.

THE FIRST GREAT AWAKENING

It was in the context of this low ebb within British Christianity that the Great Awakening took place, beginning with the formation of the Holy Club at Oxford University in 1729. This small gathering initially consisted of the Wesley brothers (John and Charles), George Whitefield as well as a few other like-minded individuals. They were soon nicknamed Methodists because of the ordered and methodical nature of their pursuit of holiness.

George Whitefield (1714–1770) preached the gospel to huge crowds in Great Britain and on several occasions crossed the Atlantic to preach in the North American colonies. While less organised than the Wesley brothers, Whitefield was greatly helped by Selena, the Countess of Huntington (1707–1791), who formed her own denomination, the Countess of Huntington Connexion, to support evangelical preachers.

John Wesley (1703–1791) was the great organiser of the revival. He gathered converts into 'classes' which would meet during the week to pray together and support one another in the faith, a precursor to the later house groups common in many churches today.[78] He was less successful in terms of his mission in North America but, shortly after returning from America, John felt that his heart was 'strangely warmed' at a meeting in Aldersgate on 24 May 1738. He therefore soon followed Whitefield's example of open-air preaching to large crowds up and down the country, albeit reluctantly at the beginning.

John's younger brother, Charles Wesley (1707–1788), was less known as a preacher but found fame as a great hymn-writer of something in the region of 7,000 hymns. Hymn-writing and singing were notable features of the revival and many of these songs, including 'O for a Thousand Tongues to Sing' and the Christmas carol 'Hark, the Herald Angels Sing', are still well known.

It is significant that the Wesley brothers were sons of a formidable woman, Susanna Wesley (1669–1742), who consequently became known as the 'Mother of Methodism'. She taught all her children for six hours per day from the age of five. They began with learning the whole alphabet on their first day and moved on to classes in Latin and Greek. Susanna would also read sermons to her children and wrote a number of commentaries on Christian belief and education, including on the Apostles' Creed and the Lord's Prayer.

In America, especially in New England, the leading

figure of the Awakening was Jonathan Edwards (1703–1758), who is also known for his writing on the subject of religious affections. There was much of this: people weeping, crying out and falling to the floor in great distress and a deep sense of their sinfulness were notable features of the revival on both sides of the Atlantic.

Disagreements about doctrine

Sadly, despite their initial unity and sense of common purpose, the key figures in the Awakening soon divided along theological lines. The main disagreement was between those who were Calvinists, such as Whitefield and Edwards, and those who were Arminians, such as the Wesleys. Compared to earlier disagreements, this dispute remained quite peaceful: the two sides published tracts and letters criticising one another, but the personal friendship between Whitefield and the Wesleys helped keep things in check. John Wesley even preached at George Whitefield's funeral. Nevertheless, this theological dispute did divide people who were essentially all wanting to preach the gospel.

Another famous preacher of the Awakening was Charles Simeon (1759–1836). Although closer in his own sympathies to Whitefield, he attempted to bring an end to the dispute by keeping on good personal terms with both sides and acting as a peacemaker. Simeon argued that the truth about the relationship between God's sovereignty and human free choice does not lie at either extreme, nor in the middle, but rather at both extremes!

There was another dividing line created by the Awakening: that between the new movement and the existing established church. While John Wesley died as a priest of the Church of England, Methodism broke away from Anglicanism following his death and became yet another denomination of Christianity, with a particular presence among working-class, industrial communities in England and Wales. This work of the Methodists among poorer communities, and the fact that many of the French Revolutionary leaders were deists or atheists, almost certainly helped prevent the spread of such violent revolution to Great Britain, despite the existence of many home-grown radical movements.

CONSEQUENCES OF THE GREAT AWAKENING

The missionary movement

One major consequence of the Great Awakening was a revival in oversees Christian missions among English-speaking Protestants. The Catholic Church had been conducting missions in Latin America, India and the Far East since the 16th century. Some missions had also been sent by continental European Protestant groups, most notably the Moravians. It was the Great Awakening, however, which gave Protestants in English-speaking countries a new urgency to become involved in the mission to take the gospel to the whole world.

William Carey (1761–1834), a Particular (that is, Calvinist) Baptist minister, was a key figure in these efforts, ultimately succeeding in forming the Baptist Missionary

Society in 1792. Carey faced some opposition from hyper-Calvinists, who thought that a sovereign God didn't require such human endeavours to save his chosen few. Nevertheless, he left for India the following year with his family, setting up missionary posts, training missionaries and translating the Bible into local languages.

Christianity had already reached India by the end of the first century but, following the Great Awakening, the influx of missionaries from the West helped swell significantly the number of Christian converts there. Unfortunately, not all later missionary activity was sympathetic to the cultural contexts of the societies in which it took place. There were a few cases, such as opposition to *suttee* (the practice of burning widows on the funeral pyre following the death of their husbands), where this intolerance had positive side effects. However, it could also lead to an unhelpful association between Christianity and European cultural preferences (and colonial interests), which left problems in the longer term.

Evangelicalism and social reform

Another positive impact of the Great Awakening was within the social sphere. While the Awakening had lost much of its fervour by the start of the 19th century, it had helped give birth to the evangelical movement within Protestant Christianity, and this was still very active in seeking to reform society.

A well-known example of this was the movement to abolish the slave trade in Great Britain. There were numerous factors at work here. For example, the slaves themselves led uprisings that made this trade in humanity increasingly unprofitable. Much also happened as a response to outrages such as the Zong massacre, where the crew of a slave ship drowned their human 'cargo' (still shackled to one other) at sea in an attempted insurance fraud. Nevertheless, much was achieved by those who mobilised public opinion against the trade, and it is notable that many of these abolitionists were Christians – often Quakers and evangelicals.

For example, Olaudah Equiano (1746–1797) was a former slave and convert to Christianity whose account of his own experiences was important in drawing attention to the stark realities of the brutal trade. In contrast, John Newton (1725–1807) was a former slave captain and Christian convert, who, eventually, became a slave abolitionist. He is well known as the writer of the lyrics to the hymn 'Amazing Grace'. Newton was able to testify to what really happened on slave ships, in opposition to the sanitised accounts of advocates of the slave trade.

Other Christians were active in running the abolitionist movement. Thomas Clarkson (1760–1846), an anti-slavery campaigner and associate of Equiano, led a grass-roots campaign against the trade, organising boycotts and raising public awareness of the evils of slavery. Some of his campaign strategies are still used today. William Wilberforce (1759–1833), an MP, led a long but ultimately successful campaign against the slave trade in Parliament.

Wilberforce was the acknowledged leader of an influential group of evangelical Christians who met in the town of Clapham (thus becoming known as the Clapham Sect) and who organised themselves according to how each member could best influence society for Christ. Thomas Clarkson was also a member of this group.

There were many others in this period who were inspired by their Christian faith to seek after change in other areas. Anthony Ashley Cooper, the Seventh Earl of Shaftesbury (1801–1885), pioneered social reforms including restrictions on child labour in mines, an upper limit of 10 hours to the length of the working day and improvements in educational provision. Elizabeth Fry (1780–1845), a Quaker, took on the unpopular campaign for reform in prisons. These early religious reformers set the stage for the great age of social reform associated with the 19th century.

The conversion testimony

One final fruit of the Great Awakening is the rise in importance of the conversion testimony as an evidence of Christianity. This new emphasis encouraged people to share their own stories of how Christ had saved them, but with it came a risk that dramatic stories, tales of sudden salvation from spectacular wickedness, could become more prominent that more commonplace accounts of coming to faith. While no doubt stirring and encouraging for many, an emphasis on such dramatic testimonies is something which can prove problematic for those, such as myself, whose stories of coming to Christ might seem somewhat more mundane and ordinary.

SUGGESTED APPLICATIONS

This historical period reminds us as Christians today of the continued importance of Jesus' Great Commission. Christ commanded us to make disciples of all nations (Matthew 28:19). Even though our attempts to reach out to our neighbours, friends, colleagues, associates, relatives and, indeed, complete strangers with the good news of Christ may not be as dramatic as what happened during the Great Awakening, nevertheless making disciples is something in which we all are instructed to be involved.

The other great application of this period is the importance of a faith which takes justice seriously. The Great Awakening resulted in concrete social change. Indeed, throughout the centuries Christians have been at the forefront of social justice and practical outreach to the poor and marginalised. The New Testament teaches that this isn't something to be seen as an added extra but rather as the fruit of a changed life (Matthew 6:1–4; 25:31–46).

None of this is easy (especially to shy, reserved, middle-class English people such as myself). There are also many pitfalls to avoid, especially if we don't want to come across as forcing ourselves and our opinions (particularly those that aren't actually part of the gospel) on others. Nor do we want to treat people as 'projects' rather than loving them. I have made both these mistakes and it seldom ends well. Yet the Great Commission comes with promises as well as commands. We are promised that 'all authority in heaven and on earth has been given to' Christ (Matthew 28:18) and that he will be with us 'always, to the very end of the age' (Matthew 28:20).

QUESTIONS FOR FURTHER STUDY

1. How can we better seek to fulfil the Great Commission to make disciples of all nations?
2. Some missionaries brought their own cultural standards and expectations with them when they went to share the gospel. Could this happen with us? How can we avoid it?
3. Do you find the dramatic conversion testimony encouraging or discouraging? Or a bit of both? Why do you feel like this?
4. How can we take social justice more seriously? What are we doing? What more can we do?

13

DOUBTS AND REVOLUTIONS

I'm sure that many of us have had moments when Christianity seemed terribly improbable. I certainly have. Equally, when I was an unbeliever, I also found that there were times when Christianity, particularly the prospect of having to account for myself to God, seemed terrifyingly likely. As C. S. Lewis once counselled, we sometimes need to ignore our changing moods.[79] Doubt isn't anything new.

THE AGE OF REASON

In more recent centuries, however, doubt about God and religion has been on the rise, particularly in the West. One major reason for this is an intellectual movement called the Enlightenment, which began in the 17th century and grew to dominate the 18th. The Enlightenment radically affected the way people in the West thought about God and the world. The focus shifted away from 'revealed religion' and 'superstition' (often seen as more or less the same thing) and towards human reason and a 'natural religion' discernible from the laws of nature.

Theology professors Grenz and Olsen describe one lasting impact of the Enlightenment as follows:

> *The Enlightenment placed humans, not God, on centre stage in history. In contrast to mediaeval and Reformation thinking, which viewed people as important largely insofar as they fit into the story of God's activity in history, Enlightenment thinkers tended to determine the importance of God in terms of his value for the story of their own lives.*[80]

As chapter eight showed, human reason had long been an important element in understanding God's ways, but now human reason was beginning to push God out of the picture altogether, or at least relegating him to the edges. Ironically, this turning away from Christianity in the West occurred at the same time as Christian missionaries were beginning to see many become believers in other parts of the world.

THE AGE OF REVOLUTIONS

This revolution in the way people thought about the world was soon matched by revolutionary changes in Western society. Three in particular stand out.

Firstly, the Industrial Revolution (which began in northern Britain in the 1750s) utterly transformed the societies of the West, and is still doing so in the developing world today. Industrialisation made the mass-production of standardised goods possible. It increased the possibilities of travel for the masses through the introduction of railway networks. It also increasingly dislocated people from the rural communities in which their families had lived for generations, as people sought opportunities in the new industrial cities. Yet it could sometimes take a while for the church to catch up with these changes.

Secondly, the American War of Independence (1775–1783) resulted in 13 British colonies in North America achieving independence as a separate nation: the United States of America. This new-found independence was important in the history of Christianity because one of the key ideological values of the new country was the separation between the state and religious institutions. This new secular arrangement radically built upon the notion of tolerance achieved in earlier centuries by abolishing the idea of state-sponsored religion altogether. The United States, therefore, provides us with an interesting example of how Christianity can continue to hold on to a large degree of cultural clout despite no longer being established by political authority. This shift towards a secular state represents one of the most important developments for Christianity since the unification of church and empire under Emperor Constantine and his successors.

Thirdly, the French Revolution of 1789 saw society turn from secularism to anti-clericalism. The church was not only to be separated from state support but to be actively driven out of the public sphere altogether. In its place some tried to elevate Deism (a belief in a philosophical 'watchmaker' God) as the new religious settlement of the country, but without much success. Christianity was therefore briefly abolished (and in some instances persecuted) within one of its former strongholds. Napoleon Bonaparte (1769–1821) brought an end to some of the excesses with a Concordat with the Catholic Church in 1801, but even now Christianity has yet to recover its former status and role in French society.

This age of revolution spread across much of the globe, being particularly fruitful in Latin America through revolutionary leaders such as Simón Bolívar (1783–1830). Liberalism, secularism and anti-clericalism became increasingly distinctive features of the new political order.

With growing industrialisation came new economic philosophies. Capitalism, with its belief in the 'invisible hand' of the free market, was expounded by Adam Smith (1723–1790) in *The Wealth of Nations*, published in 1776. Industrial capitalism, in turn, gave birth to socialism. While many socialists in Great Britain drew upon earlier radical traditions from the 17th century (many of which had Christian underpinnings), in much of the world socialism was part of the shift towards secularism and anti-clericalism. This was particularly true of those whose socialism was informed by the German theorist Karl Marx (1818–1883). In their own different ways, these new philosophies of industrial society came out of an increasingly post-Christian Europe, even though they have been co-opted by later generations of believers as part of their Christian worldview.

Another important idea which started to bear fruit in the 19th century was that of the nation state – a separate country for each people group. This concept stemmed, at least in part, from the creation of national churches at the Reformation and the increasing loss of the idea of a wider 'Christendom' to which all Christian peoples were supposedly subject. Examples of this nationalism can be seen in separatist tendencies within larger nations and empires (especially multi-national entities such as the Austro-Hungarian Empire); the growing demand for independence on the part of overseas colonies; and the Zionist movement which called for the establishment of a Jewish state in Palestine. However, many of these desires had to wait until the 20th century to find fulfilment.

AN AGE OF DOUBT

Doubts about the Bible and the supernatural

The 19th century also saw the rise of a new scepticism towards traditional understandings of the Bible, especially in Germany. The development of textual criticism subjected the biblical text to greater scrutiny than before. 'Lower' criticism confined itself largely to finding out what the real text was (especially in light of new manuscript discoveries). 'Higher' criticism, by contrast, was much more radical in its reappraisal of the Bible's meaning and authority.

As we have seen, the Enlightenment took the focus off God and instead placed it on human beings. The 19th century continued this trend with the rise of liberal theology. The most influential figure within this movement was Friedrich Schleiermacher (1768–1834). Schleiermacher's theology moved away from the authority of outside evidences such as the Scriptures and religious institutions and towards the inner sense of 'God-consciousness' within each human being – which, according to him, transcended religions.

His was a theology of feelings more than of beliefs. Even some of those who were influenced by him (such as the 20th-century Swiss theologian Karl Barth) could find themselves wondering whether Schleiermacher actually believed that God objectively existed: Barth pointedly argued against Schleiermacher that we cannot talk about God simply by talking about humans in a louder voice! Nevertheless, Schleiermacher was also important for his role in the founding of the University of Berlin in 1810, which became a model for modern research universities across Europe and beyond.

Scientific doubts

During this same period, advances in scientific discovery (such as the discovery of fossils of extinct creatures and geological evidence pointing to the vast age of the earth) too seemed increasingly to cast doubt over the truth of Scripture – at least where it was understood literally. Perhaps the best-known of these critiques is the publication in 1859 of *On the Origin of Species* by Charles Darwin (1809–

1882), which expounded the theory of evolution. This was followed in 1871 by Darwin's *The Descent of Man*, which made more explicit the idea – hinted at in *On the Origin of Species* – that human beings had evolved from apes.

Some sceptics, such as John W. Draper (1811–1882) and Andrew Dickson White (1832–1918), concluded that a 'war' existed between science and religion, which science had won, triumphing over superstition. While some of the claims made during this period (such as the idea that mediaeval thinkers believed the world to be flat)[81] have long since been debunked, this more rationalistic age resulted in divisions among Christians, which still continue, over how to respond to the new doubts and discoveries.

Revival

However, this period wasn't all doubt and gloom for the church, though there were many new questions to answer. There were further awakenings in Britain and America, involving powerful preachers such as Charles Haddon Spurgeon (1834–1892) in the UK, and Charles Grandison Finney (1792–1875) and Dwight Lyman Moody (1837–1899) in the United States. They preached the gospel to huge crowds and saw many become believers. While there is much that could be said about any of these great preachers, Finney (also a notable anti-slavery campaigner) is particularly worthy of mention since many of the familiar aspects of modern-day evangelism (such as the need to make a personal 'decision for Christ') are largely a result of his influence and innovation.

NEW RELIGIOUS MOVEMENTS

The 19th century was also a time for new religious movements, both within Christianity as well as on its margins.

'High-church' movements within Protestantism

The Oxford Movement (also known as Tractarianism) arose among Anglicans at Oxford University and spread within the Church of England beginning in 1828. This sought to return the Church of England back to its Catholic roots, with a greater emphasis on the sacraments, ceremony, iconography and music, and emphasised the authority and political independence of bishops as heirs to the apostles. The movement published 90 tracts outlining their views and helped to inspire a more mediaeval flavour to church buildings. The year after the movement began, the Catholic Emancipation Act removed almost all of the legal disqualifications on being Catholic in the UK.

The leading figure of the Oxford Movement was John Henry Newman (1801–1890), who converted to Catholicism in 1845 – along with some of his followers – and became a Catholic priest in the same year and a cardinal in 1877. Newman is particularly well-known for Tract 90, which argued that the 39 Articles of the Church of England could be understood in a Catholic sense – this led to the Anglican hierarchy suppressing the movement. Newman is also known for a teaching known as the Development of Doctrine, which argues that those Catholic beliefs which are not explicit in earlier Christianity were nevertheless valid developments from earlier roots.

A similar movement among German Calvinists, known as Mercersburg Theology, sought to revive a greater focus on the sacraments and a deeper understanding of the writings of early church fathers among Reformed Christians. While ultimately the movement made relatively little impact (as compared to the impact of the Oxford Movement on Anglicanism), it did leave lasting fruit in the publication by Philip Schaff (1819–1893) of extensive works from the church fathers and the early councils. These volumes still remain a major source of information about the early church among English-speaking Protestants.

The Salvation Army

Another important Christian movement which came into being at this time was the Salvation Army. Founded in 1865 by William Booth (1829–1912) and his wife, Catherine Booth (1829–1890), the Salvation Army was organised as a military force of soldiers of Christ, sent out to preach the gospel and minister to those in need, especially on the edges of society. From the outset, both men and women served as soldiers and officers. The army had such an impact on reducing drunkenness that a rival 'Skeleton Army' was formed in southern England (in part, it would appear, by pub landlords) to disrupt their work. There were violent clashes, with a few Salvationists being killed. Nevertheless, despite all the opposition, the Salvation Army survived and continues to thrive, now known worldwide as a major provider of social welfare and as a missionary Christian body, as well as for its strong musical tradition.

Dispensationalism

A different viewpoint emerged with the advent of Dispensationalism during the 1820s and 30s. This came into being with the founding of the Plymouth Brethren by John Nelson Darby (1800–1882), an Anglo-Irish former Anglican. It was popularised in the early 20th century by the Schofield Reference Bible and became a leading school of Bible interpretation among evangelicals, especially in the USA.

Dispensationalism divides God's workings with humanity into a series of stages or dispensations (usually seven in total), each with a different understanding of salvation. This is their framework for understanding biblical history. It distinguishes between Israel (the Jewish people) and the Christian church, both of whom are held to be God's people, but operating according to different dispensations of God's grace. It also holds strongly to the idea of a literal 1,000-year rule of Christ on the earth (the 'millennium') following Christ's second coming. Prior to this millennium, Dispensationalists believe in a seven-year tribulation during which the church is taken up into heaven, leaving Israel – with a rebuilt temple in Jerusalem – as the people of God on earth. Such belief in a literal 1,000-year rule of Christ was fairly common in the first few centuries of Christianity but the rest of Dispensationalism's framework for understanding the Bible is of more recent origin.

Movements on the margins of Christianity

The new movements we have looked at so far retained a connection with the main theological views of the early church, such as belief in the Trinity. However, as the 19th century progressed, new religious movements arose on the margins of Christianity which departed from this understanding. Many of these saw themselves as restoring the primitive faith following an apostasy of the church at the end of the first century. Perhaps the most well-known are the Mormons and the Jehovah's Witnesses, which still survive today – in large part due to their missionary zeal.

CATHOLICISM AND MODERNITY

Many movements within Christianity, such as the Salvation Army, sought new forms and expressions to meet the challenges of the age. The Catholic Church, however, entered the 19th century still seeking to resist the tide of change unleashed by the revolutionary era. As late as 1864 Pope Pius IX issued his 'Syllabus of Errors' condemning rationalism (including 'moderate rationalism'), religious tolerance, socialism, liberalism, Bible societies, secular education and other perceived ills of the modern age.

This rejection was often mutual: the Catholic Church's influence and social role was increasingly resisted by secular states. For example, in the newly united Germany, the Chancellor Otto von Bismarck (1815–1898) waged, albeit unsuccessfully, a 'culture struggle' (*Kulturkampf*) against Catholicism in German society.

The Catholic Church's next step was the calling of the First Vatican Council in 1868. This sat from 1869 to 1870 in Rome and defined the doctrine of papal infallibility, according to which the pope was protected by God from error when making a binding decision (from 'the chair of Peter') for the whole church on matters of faith or morals. Declaring the pope to be infallible (even if only under limited circumstances) was too much for some Catholics and deepened an ongoing schism. A number of Catholic churches left to ally with the 'Old Catholic' Church, who rejected exalted views of the pope's authority. Some of these breakaway churches have sought unification with Eastern Orthodoxy.

However, despite this conflict between Catholicism and modernism, the Catholic Church did become involved in the social and economic questions of the day. In 1891, a papal encyclical to the churches, entitled *Rerum Novarum* ('Of new things'), posited a third way between capitalism and socialism, known as Catholic Social Teaching. This in turn underpinned the development of Christian democratic movements.

SUGGESTED APPLICATIONS

The period from the late 18th century throughout the 19th century was an age of radical political and economic change. It saw the birth of new technologies, such as steam locomotion and the telegraph, which helped to speed up communications and travel, as well as giving birth to new economic ideologies and our modern consumerist culture. New scientific and historical discoveries raised new questions and new doubts which the church had to face, with varying degrees of success.

As inheritors of a world largely forged in these revolutionary times, how should we address the changes and doubts which they unleashed? How do believers deal with new ideas and discoveries which appear to challenge our beliefs and our understanding of the world? Rather than hiding away in holy huddles, simply encouraging doubters to keep the faith, new doubts should compel us to face and seek to answer the questions raised by the wider culture. The need for a reasoned and applied faith is one important lesson.

Another application is this: the Christian faith is robust enough not only to weather the storms thrown at it, but also to triumph even when things seem hopeless. While the 19th century was marked by doubts, it was also a time when many across the world found new hope. Christ remains the same even when the world around us seems to be in a state of perpetual change.

QUESTIONS FOR FURTHER STUDY

1 Do you think of yourself as fitting into God's story or of God as somehow fitting into yours?

2 How ought we as believers to respond to new ideas and discoveries which challenge our beliefs?

3 What are the challenges to the church today from secularism? How can we respond well?

4 In your opinion, how can the church best react to a rapidly changing world?

14

WARS AND RUMOURS OF WARS

During my time as a student in Germany I visited one of the most notorious places in modern history: Bergen-Belsen, the remnants of a Nazi concentration camp, tucked away paradoxically among peaceful villages in Lower Saxony. The Bergen-Belsen camp contains the mortal remains of over 100,000 men, women and children – mostly Jews – and stands as a silent testimony to an intentional, systematic and industrialised attempt to eradicate an entire people group from humanity.

I can still remember my visit clearly, over two decades later. I walked quietly between the mass graves then sat in silence to watch film footage of what the British soldiers found when they liberated the camp. I have had a relatively sheltered, privileged life compared with much of the world's population, and I wasn't used to coming face to face with evil – certainly not on this scale. It isn't an easy thing to forget.

AN END TO DREAMS

The 19th century can be characterised as a time when people dreamed of progress – of a new humanity forged in revolutionary overthrow of the old order, empowered by the forces of industrialisation and unshackled from the burdens of superstition to enter a new age of reason. The 20th century, by contrast, is surely the time when so many of these dreams turned into nightmares or simply came to an end. While humanity was relatively unchanged – with its old selfish, savage instinct – new technology now enabled it to both achieve new good and perpetrate new evil. This dismal verdict is perhaps not wholly fair. Nevertheless, the 20th century was surely a disappointment for many who still dreamed of the triumph of progress.

WORLD WARS AND COLD WARS

In 1914, the assassination of the Austrian Archduke Franz Ferdinand in Sarajevo by Gavrilo Princip, a Serbian nationalist, triggered a series of events which would lead to the mechanised slaughter of the First World War. Millions of people died in this war, which was followed by a worldwide epidemic of influenza that killed many millions more.

The First World War was one of the most significant events of the 20th century. Out of it flowed the Russian Revolution and the rise of both Communism and Fascism as governing ideologies. New countries were created – Yugoslavia, Syria, Iraq and Palestine – which would come again to prominence before the century concluded. Most notably, the First World War, especially the terms of the Treaty of Versailles that ended it, helped lay the seeds of discontent and economic collapse in Germany. This in turn led to the rise of National Socialism and the Second World War.

Many pages could be filled listing the horrors and tragedies of the 20th century, so far the bloodiest in our history. The technological advances which began in the 19th century did make a positive impact: they utterly transformed sanitation, communications and transportation, leading to previously unimaginable advances in human wellbeing. They also, however, led to mechanised warfare, the use of gas chambers and the atom bomb. For decades after the end of the Second World War, rival nuclear powers faced each other, waiting nervously on the precipice of mutually assured destruction. Even though the Cold War is technically over, the nuclear weapons remain and we still sit on that precipice.

THE JEWISH STATE AND THE END OF THE WORLD

Following the destruction of the Jewish temple by the Romans in AD 70, many Jews moved to Central and Eastern Europe. There they lived (facing opposition and sporadic violence) for almost two millennia. In the 19th century, many of these Jewish populations began to win greater civil rights. Yet in the middle of the 20th century, in the very heart of civilised Europe, they began to be systematically exterminated. Something in the region of six million Jews died in Nazi camps (alongside a further five million people who differed from the Nazi ideal in other ways).[82]

Not surprisingly, many European Jews who survived the Second World War didn't wish to stay in Europe, even when countries desired this. Sometimes they weren't wanted – the defeat of Nazism didn't end anti-Semitism. This near destruction of the Jewish population of Europe galvanised world opinion in the direction of what the Zionists had been dreaming of for decades: the establishment of a Jewish State in Palestine. In 1948, therefore, Palestine was partitioned and a new state of Israel created as a national homeland for the Jews.

The birth (or, some might say, rebirth) of the state of Israel was seen by a number of Christians as being a fulfilment of biblical prophecy. Books began to appear, especially in the 1980s, which argued that Christ's return was likely to take place sometime around 1988, that being one biblical generation, or 40 years, after Israel's restoration to their homeland. Needless to say, this 'end-times panic' was in vain: Christ didn't return in 1988 and bring down the curtain on history – somewhat fortunately for me, since I became a Christian in the post-non-apocalyptic disappointment of 1989! Sadly, though, this failure to appreciate that no one knows the day or the hour of Christ's return hasn't stopped similar prophecies being made since.

PERMISSIVE SOCIETY AND CULTURE WARS

The 20th century was also a time of great social change and social conflict. Both the two World Wars saw a breakdown in traditional sexual morals, especially those which limited sexual intercourse to marriage or even to a committed relationship. Even the relative conservatism of the 1950s could be understood as a reaction to what had been going on during the war.

It was during the 1960s and 70s, though – as the children of the post-war baby boom began to shift the demographic balance in favour of the young – that the legislative framework within many Western nations was altered to reflect the new moral sensibilities. Homosexuality was legalised and the (often barbaric) attempts at medical 'cures' for this discontinued. Contraception became widely available and abortion was made legal in many countries. The censorship of pornography was relaxed. Of course, these changes weren't simply about sex, drugs and rock and roll, nor only concerned with ethical questions about the sanctity (or otherwise) of human life. This was also a time for challenging hypocrisy, addressing the risk of ecological catastrophe and standing up against racial and other social injustices.

In response to some of these dramatic social changes, especially those relating to human life and sexuality, came the culture wars and the rise of the religious right.[83] These have become particularly notable in North America from the 1980s onwards, as many Christians have sought to redirect society morally through political power. I would suggest, though, that this political route has not been quite as successful in changing laws and social attitudes as many of its proponents would have wished. Some may feel that there has not been sufficient emphasis in some of these campaigns on issues of social justice. Moreover, partisan politics has opened the door to many temptations, especially that of keeping at a distance from (or even demonising) perceived opponents. I am not saying that Christians should stay out of public life – far from it. (I have myself been a member of the Movement for Christian Democracy). However, in all our activism, we should always remember that we do not wrestle 'against flesh and blood' (Ephesians 6:12). We are not called to hate. Our fight is not against other people.

RENEWAL, REFORM AND REUNION

The 20th century was in many ways marked by conflict but there were still glimmerings of restored hope for greater renewal, unity and peace.

A new Pentecost?

Renewal was seen in the 20th century with the rise of the Pentecostal and charismatic movements. These emphasised the ongoing reality of the gifts of the Holy Spirit, especially speaking in tongues and prophecy. The movement began in 1906 with a revival centred around the Azuza Street Mission in Los Angeles, USA. Some charismatic Christians formed their own denominations;

others chose to operate within the structures of existing churches, including the Catholic Church. They often led to a search for a wider renewal or 'restoration' of the church, desiring something more akin to that in Acts 2.

Many of these claims were, and are, very controversial indeed. Although the controversy over the gifts of the Spirit has cooled in more recent decades, it hasn't entirely gone away. Charismatic renewal did bring radical change to many churches and led to a renewed focus on the person and work of the third person of the Trinity. However, in some cases the manifestations of this movement (such as people falling over, or making animal noises) could appear a bit odd.[84]

The Second Vatican Council

It would not be too much of an exaggeration to see the Second Vatican Council, opened in 1962 by Pope Paul XXIII, as ushering in Roman Catholicism's modern relationship with the world. The council accepted Protestants as 'separated brethren' and rejected the idea that the Catholic Church should seek, where possible, the support of the state in its mission. In other words, as historian Bruce Shelley puts it, 'Roman Catholicism solemnly renounced in principle any use of external force against the voice of conscience.'[85] Vatican II, as it was informally known, led to subsequent changes, such as services being held in contemporary languages rather than in Latin. These reforms remain controversial among more conservative Catholics, but their importance is hard to understate.

The ecumenical movement

Running alongside this reform within the Catholic Church was a much wider desire between Christians for reunion. One example of this search for unity is the World Council of Churches, which was formed in 1948 and includes representatives from many churches and denominations (though not yet the Catholic Church). While there are many convictions which Christians have in common – most of all our shared love for the Lord Jesus Christ – there is always the risk, or fear, that these attempts at unity could result in a lowest-common-denominator form of Christianity in which important truths are compromised in the search for peace. Dialogue about our differences and how to resolve them, however, is surely a good thing.

An alternative approach is for different church bodies to come together in support of common goals, for example as in the 1974 International Congress on World Evangelisation at Lausanne, Switzerland. Indeed, even the religious right and similar political movements could be understood in terms of Christians coming together to face common concerns. The crises faced by humanity in the 20th century seemed to cry out for a more united Christian response.

SUGGESTED APPLICATIONS

It has been difficult to write this chapter without getting bogged down in controversies, some of which are still very much live issues. What then can we learn from the experience of the 20th century, with all its fighting?

We should keep in mind that we are still very much the same creatures as our ancestors were: fallen human beings. The 20th century saw the deaths of tens of millions of people through war and genocide, despite all the dreams of a better tomorrow. (It is notable that the decline in religious belief and superstition in the West didn't reduce the bloodshed; not all wars are caused by religion after all). Fundamentally, humanity hasn't changed much even if our social organisation is different and our technology vastly improved. We would be wise to remember who we are and what we are capable of, and to stay vigilant.

Another important lesson is how to engage well with our culture and our society for the sake of the good news of Jesus Christ. We should learn how to be engaged in the public sphere and to stand up for our beliefs and values while also being wary of the allure and the danger of political power, especially its ability to demonise others. In short, we must learn to be more like our Lord Jesus Christ: 'full of grace and truth' (John 1:14).

QUESTIONS FOR FURTHER STUDY

1 Are we, do you think, fundamentally the same as our ancestors? If not, how have we changed?

2 What is your view of the charismatic movement and the gifts of the Holy Spirit? What impact do you think this movement has had on the wider church?

3 What should be the Christian attitude to politics? How can we make good use of the opportunities of becoming involved in politics while resisting the temptations that this involvement can bring?

4 Many Christian believers have served in the armed forces throughout the centuries. Others have argued that Christianity teaches pacifism. In your view, what should be the Christian attitude to war? Is there such a thing as a just war?

5 How likely, in your view, is greater unity between different denominations of Christians? Is this even something desirable?

15

WHERE NOW?

The human race, to which so many of my readers belong, has been playing at children's games from the beginning, and will probably do it till the end, which is a nuisance for the few people who grow up. And one of the games to which it is most attached is called 'Keep to-morrow dark' … The players listen very carefully and respectfully to all that the clever men have to say about what is to happen in the next generation. The players then wait until all the clever men are dead, and bury them nicely. Then they go and do something else.[86]

These witty words, by G. K. Chesterton (from the first chapter of his curious novel *The Napoleon of Notting Hill*) are a warning against what I am about to do: to hazard an educated guess at what the future might hold for the church. This is, after all, supposed to be an introduction to history rather than an attempt at prophecy. Nevertheless, it might be worth taking a peek at a few current trends which may have an impact on the future of the faith. Time will tell whether I am right or wrong.

GLOBAL CHRISTIANITY

Firstly, while the focus of this book has been on the Middle East, Europe and, to a lesser extent, North America, it is worth acknowledging that Christianity has long been an international faith. Churches were established in India, North Africa and parts of the Far East long before the missionary movements of the 16th to 20th centuries. These, in turn, saw the Christian faith spread to more parts of the world than ever before.

This has happened to such an extent that it is now far more likely for someone to encounter a Christian believer in South America, sub-Saharan Africa or parts of South East Asia than in the Middle East or Western Europe. The demographic balance of Christianity has shifted south and east; it is no longer a Western religion. Indeed many Western countries are now being evangelised by believers from communities who were themselves recipients of Western missionary activity in centuries gone by. It doesn't seem unreasonable to suppose, therefore, that we will continue to see greater cultural diversity and difference in the way in which the faith is expressed and communicated.

RELIGIOUS CONFLICT AND EXTREMISM

Secondly, it became apparent even before the 20th century was laid to rest that religious conflict hasn't gone away. Instead religious extremism – particularly the threats posed by radical Islamists, but also those from others on the extremes of the political spectrum (some of whom may claim to be acting in the name of Christianity) – is now a regular feature of our news broadcasts. How are we to react? Should we be afraid? Should we allow ourselves to be filled with anger and hatred? How can we learn to love our enemies (Matthew 5:43–45) in such a climate, when our own faith potentially makes us suspicious even to our friends and neighbours? This has always been a hard ask. It doesn't look as though it's going to get any easier.

CHRISTIANITY IN THE INFORMATION AGE

Finally, the Internet and social media in general present many opportunities, as well as challenges and temptations, for the believer. Current generations now have access to more information, and more quickly, than any other human beings who have ever lived. Far from being ignorant, we are in danger of being overwhelmed. The challenge for us now is to sift and discern the true from the false; the useful from the useless; the vital from the trivial.

We have more opportunity to learn about each other and this world we share than ever before. This is a positive implication of the growing connectedness of the world online. It is now much more difficult for Christians across the world to remain ignorant of one another's faith and practice. There are greater opportunities for unity and understanding among believers than has been the case for a long time. Nevertheless, we need the wisdom to use these possibilities well.

A VISION FOR OUR CHURCH

The question remains where do we go from here? There are lots of different ideas about the future of the church. Some, wanting to reach out to those who have lost their faith in the church (though not necessarily in Jesus), have sought a more informal, less institutional expression of Christianity. Some, at the other extreme, want to rebuild Christendom, seeing political power and influence as a means to establish the lordship of Jesus Christ over society and reshape the culture.

I am wary of both these approaches. On the one hand, Christ died to establish the church, so I do not believe that he wants us to give up on her, however much we may mourn the fact that she hasn't often lived up to her high calling, and has left many hurt and wounded. On the other hand, I remain unconvinced by the allure of using political power to re-establish Christian influence in society. Jesus' kingdom is not of this world (John 18:36). Jesus does not call his servants to fight perceived enemies, as people did during the Crusades, but to lay down our lives in service for them. The devil tempted Christ with the allure of power, with all the kingdoms of the world and their splendour, and Jesus overcame him (Matthew 4:8–9). Let us, as his followers, do likewise.

What should we do then? I would answer: build the church; make disciples of all nations; learn what it means to be the body of Christ in our society (including in public life); serve others, even loving our enemies. It's a difficult and challenging message, and not one that I would have come up with if I were inventing a religion to suit myself, but I do believe that it is what the Bible teaches.

My hope, then, is for a church which is rooted in the past without being closed to the present. A church which keeps its family traditions but does so with joy that wouldn't be out of place at a wedding. A church which holds on firmly to the faith for which many martyrs gave their lives, but which does so humbly, being prepared to listen and to make sure that it understands what others are really saying. A church which has done some hard thinking and is able to give answers to tough questions (as well as reassurance to those who are doubting), but which would rather win people than win secondary arguments. A holy church, a prophetic witness to the world, but also a welcoming home to those seeking forgiveness. A church which doesn't seek to fight other people but to love them and point them to Christ. A church which knows itself to be the family of Christ and which shows the family likeness. May God give us grace, in all our weakness, to build and to be such a church.

QUESTIONS FOR FURTHER STUDY

1 What do you think could be the impact on the local church of Christianity becoming more global and more culturally diverse?

2 How can we obey Jesus' command to love our enemies in an age of terrorism and ideological extremism?

3 Where do we find the wisdom to help us discern and process the vast amounts of information to which we now have access?

4 How can we build, and be, a church which looks more like Jesus?

TIMELINE

The following timeline might be helpful in assisting the reader to relate the events covered in this book to each other and to other events in history. All dates are AD (or, if you prefer, CE). Where exact dates are uncertain, I have given approximations.

Year	Event
c. 95	Completion of the New Testament.
c. 96	The letter 1 Clement, possibly the earliest of the works of the Apostolic Fathers, is written.
c. 98–117	Martyrdom of Ignatius of Antioch.
c. 150	Justin Martyr writes his *First Apology for the Christians.*
c. 155	Martyrdom of Polycarp of Smyrna.
c. 180	Irenaeus of Lyons writes *Against Heretics.*

c. 202–203	Martyrdom of Perpetua and her companions. Prior to her death, Perpetua wrote a prison diary which is among the few surviving first-hand accounts from an early Christian martyr.
c. 225	The *Apostolic Tradition* of Hippolytus of Rome records an early liturgy used in Christian worship.
250	Edict of Decius starts an empire-wide persecution of Christians, opening up a debate in the church as to whether those who renounced their faith to avoid persecution can be restored to salvation.
313	Constantine the Great issues the Edict of Milan, legalising Christianity in the Roman Empire.
c. 318	Athanasius of Alexandria writes *On the Incarnation.*
325	First Council of Nicaea defends the eternal divinity of Christ as one who is of the 'same being' as the Father.
348	Death of Pachomius the Great.
356	Death of Anthony the Great.

361	Julian the Apostate becomes emperor, briefly restoring Roman paganism as the official religion of Rome.
367	Athanasius's 39th Festal Letter lists the 27 acknowledged books of the New Testament.
381	Theodosius I makes Christianity the official religion of the Roman Empire.
381	First Council of Constantinople defends the divinity of the Son and of the Holy Spirit.
410	Sack of Rome by the Goths.
412	Condemnation of Coelestius, a disciple of Pelagius, by a synod at Carthage in North Africa.
430	Death of Augustine of Hippo.
431	Council of Ephesus condemns Nestorianism.
451	Council of Chalcedon issues the Definition of Chalcedon, defining the relationship between the divinity and humanity of Christ.
455	Sack of Rome by the Vandals.
476	Romulus Augustulus, the last Roman emperor in the West, is deposed.
529	Council of Orange condemns Semi-Pelagianism.

543	Death of Benedict of Nursia, a leading figure in the development of monasticism in the West.
553	Second Council of Constantinople condemns ongoing Nestorian and Eutychian views of Christ, as well as ideas about reincarnation and universalism attributed to the third-century Christian writer, Origen.
596	Pope Gregory the Great sends Augustine of Canterbury on a mission to convert the English to Christianity.
622	Mohammed flees from Mecca to Medina (the starting point of the Muslim calendar).
663	Synod of Whitby agrees the date of Easter, ending a dispute between Celtic and Anglo-Saxon Christianity.
680	Third Council of Constantinople condemns monotheletism (the idea that Christ has no independent human will).
787	Second Council of Nicaea defends the veneration of images against the actions of 'iconoclasts' (image-breakers).
800	Charlemagne crowned Holy Roman Emperor, founding a new empire in the West.

863–9	Cyril and Methodius translate the Bible into Old Church Slavonic, paving the way for the conversion of the Slavs to Christianity.
988	The Rus of Kiev formally convert to Christianity.
c. 1000	Leif Erikson sails to America.
1054	The Great Schism between Eastern and Western Christianity occurs.
1059	Decree on Papal Elections first establishes the process whereby the pope is elected by cardinals.
1066	Battle of Hastings.
1093	Anselm appointed Archbishop of Canterbury.
1095	Pope Urban II calls for the Crusades, known for their cry, *Deus Vult!* (If God wills it!)
1096–1102	The First Crusade.
1099	Jerusalem captured by the crusaders.
1120	Foundation of the Knights Templar.
1144	Fall of Edessa to the Muslims.
1145	Pope Eugenius III calls for the Second Crusade.

1147–9	The Second Crusade.
1158	World's first university in Bologna granted imperial privileges.
1187	Jerusalem captured by Saladin.
1189–92	The Third Crusade.
1202–04	The Fourth Crusade.
1204	Sack of Constantinople by crusaders.
1209–29	The Albigensian Crusade in the South of France.
1212	The Children's Crusade.
1215	Magna Carta.
1217–29	The Fifth Crusade.
1223	The monastic 'rule' of Francis of Assisi is established.
1229	Frederick II becomes the ruler of Jerusalem.
1244	Recapture of Jerusalem by Muslims.
1272	Earliest mention of a mechanical clock, invented by monks.
1274	Death of Thomas Aquinas.
1274	Second Council of Lyons attempts to reunify the Catholic and Orthodox churches.

1291	Fall of Acre.
1312	Order of the Knights Templar is suppressed.
1325	Peter, Metropolitan of Moscow and all Russia, moves the capital of the Church of Rus (Russia) to Moscow.
1347	First appearance of the Black Death in Europe – a plague which would kill about a third of the population.
1384	Death of John Wycliffe.
1401	The Act *De Haeretico Comburendo* permits the burning of heretics at the stake in England.
1414–18	Council of Constance ends the Western Schism in the papacy.
1415	Jan Hus burnt at the stake.
1439–45	Council of Ferrara-Florence attempts to reunite the Catholic and Orthodox churches.
1453	Fall of Constantinople to the Turks.
1455	Johann Gutenberg prints the Bible using moveable type.
1492	Columbus sails across the Atlantic.

1516	Desiderius Erasmus publishes the first printed Greek New Testament.
1517	Martin Luther sparks the Protestant Reformation by issuing his 95 theses against the sale of indulgences.
1520	Martin Luther excommunicated.
1521	Martin Luther defends his views at the Diet of Worms.
1522	Martin Luther publishes his translation of the New Testament into German.
1526	William Tyndale publishes his first translation of the New Testament into English.
1530	Confession of Augsburg proclaims Lutheran doctrine.
1531	Death of Ulrich Zwingli.
1534	Act of Supremacy makes Henry VIII Supreme Head of the Church of England.
1536	First edition of John Calvin's *Institutes of the Christian Religion*.
1536	Deaths of Erasmus and William Tyndale.
1540	Ignatius Loyola founds the Jesuits.

1543	Nicholas Copernicus publishes *On the Revolutions of the Heavenly Spheres*, which argues that the earth orbits the sun.
1545–63	Council of Trent clarifies Catholic doctrine following the Reformation and brings an end to abuses such as the selling of indulgences.
1546	Death of Martin Luther.
1552	Jesuits begin missionary activity to Asia.
1553	Michael Servetus burned at the stake in Geneva.
1555	The Peace of Augsburg establishes legal co-existence between Catholics and Protestants in Germany and Austria.
1559	Queen Elizabeth I's Act of Uniformity establishes the English Book of Common Prayer as the church's liturgy.
1560	Geneva Bible is published.
1564	Death of John Calvin.
1570	Excommunication of Queen Elizabeth I of England.
1571	39 Articles of Religion define the doctrines of the Church of England.

1588	Spanish Armada launched against England.
1598	The Edict of Nantes grants religious toleration to Protestants in France.
1609	Death of James Arminius.
1610	Arminian Remonstrance is published in the Netherlands.
1611	Publication of the King James Version of the Bible.
1616	The Catholic Church condemns the works of Copernicus.
1618	Beginning of the Thirty Years' War in Germany.
1633	Galileo Galilei put on trial in Rome.
1642	Outbreak of Civil War in Great Britain.
1643	The Solemn League and Covenant is signed in Scotland and the Westminster Confession of Faith (a leading Calvinist confession) is drawn up in England.
1648	The Peace of Westphalia ends the Thirty Years' War, and accepts freedom of worship for Protestants in Germany, Switzerland and the Netherlands.
1649	Execution of King Charles I.

1653	Oliver Cromwell becomes Lord Protector.
1655	Jews are permitted to return to Britain, four centuries after they were expelled.
1660	Restoration of the Monarchy in Britain.
1661–65	The Clarendon Code re-establishes the Church of England and restricts religious practice for non-Anglican Protestants.
1683	Turkish armies defeated at the gates of Vienna.
1685	Edict of Nantes revoked, renewing the persecution of the Huguenots (Protestants) in France.
1688	James II overthrown in the Glorious Revolution.
1689	Act of Toleration extends civil liberty in Britain to non-Anglican Protestants.
1707	Union of England and Scotland, forming the United Kingdom of Great Britain.
1730s	Start of the First Great Awakening.
1741	Jonathan Edwards preaches the sermon 'Sinners in the Hands of an Angry God'.
1770	Death of George Whitefield.

1775–83	American War of Independence.
1776	Adam Smith publishes *The Wealth of Nations,* a foundational text of free-Market capitalism.
1789	The French Revolution begins.
1791	Death of John Wesley.
1793	William Carey sails to India as a missionary.
1801	Union between Great Britain and Ireland.
1804	Napoleon crowned Emperor of the French.
1815	Napoleon defeated at the Battle of Waterloo.
1829	Catholic Emancipation Act is passed in Great Britain.
1841	Tract 90, the last of the Oxford Movement's 'Tracts for the Times', is published, arguing that the 39 Articles of the Church of England could be interpreted in a Catholic sense.
1848	*The Communist Manifesto* published by Karl Marx and Friederich Engels.
1854	Doctrine of the Immaculate Conception of Mary confirmed by the Catholic Church as dogma.

1859	Charles Darwin publishes *On the Origin of Species.*
1864	The papal *Syllabus of Errors* opposes modernism.
1865	China Inland Mission founded by Hudson Taylor.
1870	The First Vatican Council establishes papal infallibility as dogma.
1871	Charles Darwin publishes *The Descent of Man.*
1884	Revised Version of the Bible published.
1891	The papal encyclical *Rerum Novarum* lays out the social teaching of the Catholic Church.
1899–1901	Boxer rebellion in China attacks foreign influences, including Christianity.
1906	Azuza Street Revival begins the Pentecostal movement.
1912	The Titanic sinks on its maiden voyage.
1914	Assassination of Archduke Franz Ferdinand of Austria.
1914–18	First World War.
1917	The Russian Revolution.
1922	Partition of Ireland.

1930	Anglican Lambeth Conference accepts the use of contraception within marriage as valid.
1933	Adolf Hitler becomes Chancellor of Germany.
1934	Adolf Hitler makes himself *Führer* (Leader) of Germany following the death of President von Hindenburg.
1937	The Rape of Nanking by Japanese troops.
1938	*Anschluss* ('union') of Germany and Austria.
1939–45	Second World War.
1941	Japanese attack American naval base at Pearl Harbor, leading to the USA entering the Second World War.
1945	Invention and use of the atomic bomb.
1945	Establishment of the United Nations.
1948	Creation of the State of Israel.
1948	Establishment of the World Council of Churches.
1950	Doctrine of the Assumption of the Virgin Mary confirmed as dogma by the Catholic Church.
1955–75	Vietnam War.

1960	The contraceptive pill approved for use in the USA; trials begin in the UK with the pill being approved the following year.
1962–65	Second Vatican Council.
1963	Martin Luther King Jr writes his 'Letter from Birmingham Jail'.
1968	Papal encyclical *Humanae Vitae* ('On human life') reaffirms Catholic opposition to abortion and contraception.
1969	Neil Armstrong walks on the moon.
1974	International Congress on World Evangelisation.
1979	Iranian revolution.
1981	HIV clinically diagnosed for the first time.
1989–90	Fall of Communism in Eastern Europe.
1990	Invention of the World Wide Web.
1999	Joint Declaration on Justification by representatives of the Catholic and Lutheran churches offers the possibility of mutual understanding between the two churches on this central doctrine of the Reformation.

SUGGESTIONS FOR FURTHER READING

Here are a few suggestions for books which might help you take the next steps in reconnecting with the history of the church.

In terms of broader histories of the church, Bruce L. Shelley's *Church History in Plain Language* (fourth edition Thomas Nelson, 2013) is a reasonably comprehensive and accessible account from an American perspective.

A somewhat older book which is still worth reading as an introduction to the early centuries of Christian history is F. F. Bruce, *The Spreading Flame* (revised edition Send the Light, 1958). Bruce starts in the first century with the ministry of the Apostle Paul to the Corinthian church and traces the history of the church up to the conversion of the English in the seventh century.

Michael Reeves, *The Breeze of the Centuries* (IVP, 2010) provides a more detailed introduction to the thought of some of the early theologians mentioned in this book, with chapters on the Apostolic Fathers, Justin Martyr, Irenaeus of Lyons, Athanasius of Alexandria, Augustine of Hippo, Anselm of Canterbury and Thomas Aquinas. Michael Reeves' book is particularly helpful in providing suggestions for you to start reading the writings of these influential theologians for yourself.

Great Christian Thinkers – a Starter Kit by Colin Blakely (SPCK, 2000) provides a good introduction to the life and thought of a great number of Christian thinkers, ordered alphabetically from Abelard to Zwingli. These brief introductions are also very accessible, being both short and often funny.

In terms of books which relate to specific chapters, I would also like to recommend the following:

A good starting point for understanding the theological disputes at the Council of Nicaea would be to read Athanasius, *On the Incarnation*, in which he summarises some of his key beliefs. The Fig Books translation (2013) is pretty accessible and features a wonderful introduction by C. S. Lewis. On a personal note, I am deeply indebted to this book, which helped restore my faith after a long and dark period in my life.

David Bentley-Taylor, *The Apostle from Africa: The Life and Thought of Augustine of Hippo* (Christian Focus, 2002) is a good introduction to the life and theology of the only character in this book to get a chapter all to himself. In terms of getting to grips with Augustine's own writings, I would highly recommend, at the very least, that Christians read his *Confessions* for themselves. Hendrickson's Christian Classics have published a translation in English (2004), although some readers might find the language used rather old-fashioned.

Jonathan Phillips, *Holy Warriors: A Modern History of the Crusades* (Vintage, 2010) has been very helpful to me in giving a good, detailed overview of this controversial area of Christian history, and is very balanced in its approach. There is a lot of material out there about the Crusades, as people continue to be interested in the period and its legacy today.

When it comes to the history of religion and science and the scholarship of the Christian Middle Ages, the go-to book, in my opinion, is James Hannam's excellent work, *God's Philosophers: How the Medieval World Laid the Foundations of Modern Science* (Icon, 2009). For more information on the debate about Columbus and the mistaken idea that mediaeval people believed the world to be flat, I would also strongly recommend Jeffrey B. Russell, *Inventing the Flat Earth: Columbus and Modern Historians* (new edition Praeger, 1997).

Regarding the Protestant Reformation, Michael Reeves, *The Unquenchable Flame* (second edition IVP, 2016) is a good overview from a strongly pro-Reformation perspective. For readers looking for an alternative, critical approach, Archpriest Josiah Trenham, *Rock and*

Sand: An Orthodox Appraisal of the Protestant Reformers and their Teachings (Newrome Press, 2015) gives a less pro-Reformation perspective from the standpoint of Eastern Orthodox Christianity.

Concerning primary sources for the Reformation, The Augsburg Confession is available online and is a good summary of where early Lutherans agreed and disagreed with the Catholic Church. Those who wish to make a start in understanding Calvinism but do not have the time or the discipline to work their way through John Calvin's epic systematic theology, *Institutes of the Christian Religion* (available in a large two-volume set from the Westminster Press, 1960), will doubtless be delighted to hear that Calvin produced a short introductory work in 1537 called *Instruction in Faith* (also available from the Westminster Press, 1977). In this much more accessible work, he outlines his core theology for the citizens of Geneva in 33 short chapters (some less than a page long!).

John Pollock has produced a number of excellent warts-and-all biographies of Christian figures, including John Wesley, George Whitefield and John Newton, which are a good place to start reading about the Great Awakening of the 18th century.

Finally, those looking to start reading the primary source material for themselves could do worse than begin with Henry Bettenson and Chris Maunder (eds) *Documents of the Christian Church* (fourth edition OUP, 2011), which gives selected readings from Christian documents from the end of the first century right up into the 20th century.

ENDNOTES

1. The Early Church

1. The word 'martyr' comes from a Greek word meaning 'witness' – the martyrs were those who bore witness that Christ meant more to them than life itself.

2. There is also a document called 2 Clement, an early sermon on the importance of repentance, but this was almost certainly written by a different author.

3. At one point Clement even refers to the myth of the phoenix as an example of resurrection, calling the Corinthian Christians to live like those whom Christ had raised from spiritual death.

4. This teaching was known as 'Docetism' from the Greek word *dokein*, meaning 'to seem'.

5. The sixth of these commandments teaches that each human being is accompanied through life by an angel (on the right) and a demon (on the left), who attempt to lead their human subject towards choosing virtue or vice respectively, an idea since picked up by cartoons.

[6] There is also a *Second Apology*, written by Justin Martyr, in response to a specific outrage against a Christian woman who was denounced by her pagan husband and put to death. Among Justin's other works, one of the most notable is an account of a debate with a Jewish philosopher: the *Dialogue with Trypho*.

[7] Irenaeus of Lyons, *Against Heresies,* book 1, chapter 11, section 4.

[8] The early church's Old Testament also included some books which are not accepted by Jews or most Protestants as inspired. Arguments about the authority of these additional books (known as the Deuterocanonical books or Apocrypha) continue to this day.

[9] These alternative accounts sometimes reflect a Gnostic belief that Jesus wasn't actually human, for example as in the *Acts of John*, chapter 93, where his body is sometimes solid and sometimes immaterial, and his feet don't touch the ground!

2. Worship

[10] The 'Ruler' is possibly the local bishop.

[11] See, for example, Hippolytus of Rome, *The Apostolic Tradition*, written in the third century. Hippolytus was a fairly conservative writer and his description of Christian worship probably looks back to an earlier time.

[12] The *Didache* 7:1–3.

[13] Justin Martyr, *First Apology*, chapter 61.

[14] 'Eucharist' comes from the Greek word for 'giving thanks'.

[15] Ignatius of Antioch, *To the Smyrneans*, 6:2.

[16] Justin Martyr, *First Apology*, chapter 66.

[17] Irenaeus of Lyons, *Against Heresies*, book 2, chapter 32, section 4.

[18] The Montanists included (in his later years) the third-century Christian writer Tertullian.

3. God in Three Persons

[19] In fact this was neither written by Athanasius nor a creed.

[20] Irenaeus of Lyons, *Against Heresies*, book 4, chapter 20, section 1 – my emphasis.

[21] 'Ecumenical' comes from a Greek word meaning 'household', thus seeing the different churches as parts of a single family. An ecumenical council is a council of church leaders representing the consensus of the church as a whole.

[22] This symbol would have been either the cross or the 'chi-rho'. The latter comes from the Greek letters 'chi' (X) and 'rho' (P), the first two letters (in Greek) of the word 'Christ'.

[23] The Council of Jerusalem decided that Gentiles (non-Jews) did not have to accept circumcision and Jewish dietary laws in order to become Christians.

[24] A later tradition puts the number at 318.

[25] A longer version of this creed, known as the Nicene Creed, is still read at Sunday worship in many churches today.

[26] See 'Making and begetting', the first chapter of book four of C. S. Lewis' *Mere Christianity* (first published Geoffrey Bles, 1952) for more on this idea.

[27] All of the cities named here are in what is now Turkey.

[28] Interestingly both the synagogue and the third-century house church in Dura Europos had paintings and other images of Bible stories on their walls.

[29] Gregory Nazianzen, epistle 101: 'Critique of Apollinarius and Apollinarianism'.

[30] Some readers may suspect that a few words have been left out here. The addition of the words 'and the Son' to this final part of the Nicene Creed, and the controversy (and subsequent division of the church) which this caused, is covered in chapter 5.

[31] Peter Kreeft, *Fundamentals of the Faith* (Ignatius, 1990), chapter 19.

4. Into the Wilderness

[32] Anthony the Great's name is also spelled as Antony.

33 Athanasius, *The Life of St. Anthony*, chapter 2 – though the language has been slightly modernised. By chapter 3, the little amount which Anthony had kept for his sister was also given to the poor, following another similar experience of going into church and hearing Matthew 6:34 being read. Anthony's sister (who, sadly, isn't named anywhere in Athanasius's work) was handed over to a community of nuns and ultimately became their head.

34 The 'desert mothers' include Amma Syncletica and Theodora of Alexandria, whose sayings are recorded alongside those of the 'desert fathers'.

35 The work 'monk' ultimately derives from the Greek word *monos*, meaning 'alone'.

36 I do not wish in any way to diminish the vital importance of the works of Muslim scholars, many of which found their way into Europe from the 12th century onwards. They not only helped acquaint European scholars with the writings of the Islamic world (and beyond), but in many cases provided them greater access to the works of ancient Greek writers, which had been lost to the West.

37 G. K. Chesterton, 'The Secret People' (1907).

5. A Restless Heart

[38] Augustine of Hippo is not to be confused with Augustine of Canterbury, who helped bring Christianity to the south of England during the seventh century.

[39] See chapter 4 for more about the life and work of Anthony.

[40] Here Augustine is quoting Romans 13:13–14. The translation used is similar to the King James Version.

[41] Augustine, *Confessions*, 8.12.

[42] See Augustine's 'Letter 93 to Vincentius' for some of his arguments as to why he thought that this sort of coercion might be acceptable.

[43] Augustine, *The City of God Against the Pagans*, book 14, chapter 28.

[44] These definitions are taken from Barclay M. Newman, *A Concise Greek–English Dictionary of the New Testament* (revised edition Hendrickson, 2010).

[45] Augustine, *Confessions*, 10.29.

[46] Augustine, *Faith, Hope and Charity*, chapter 9. This book is also known as the *Enchiridion* – a small handbook.

[47] 'Double predestination' is the idea that, prior to sin entering the world, God predetermined that certain people would be saved and that certain people would be damned, before any of them had done either good or evil.

6. Torn Apart

[48] These groups are sometimes called the 'Oriental Orthodox' churches.

[49] It is from this group that we get the word 'vandalism' in English.

[50] This was especially so during the reign of Pope Gregory the Great (590–604).

7. Holy War

[51] Technically, Philip II of France was the leader of the Third Crusade, but Richard the Lionheart, his second-in-command, was the one who more effectively captured the popular imagination.

[52] Emperor Frederick II's rule was made easier by his fluent Arabic and cultural sensitivity, not features shared by too many of his fellow crusaders, it would seem.

8. Mediaeval Wisdom

[53] Note that being ignorant is not the same thing as being irrational.

[54] Claudius Ptolemy, *Almagest*, book 1, chapter 4.

[55] Claudius Ptolemy, *Almagest*, book 1, chapter 6.

[56] Logic was a big deal for educated people in the Middle Ages. A popular activity at mediaeval

universities was for students to think up difficult (often bizarre) problems for their tutors to try to answer through their powers of reasoning. It would seem, however, that no one ever actually asked the supposed question of how many angels could dance on the head of a pin!

[57] This is also known as the *Summa Theologiae* ('summary of theology').

[58] James Hannam, *God's Philosophers* (Icon, 2010), p. 299.

[59] Daniel J. Boorstin, *The Discoverers* (Vintage, 1983), chapter 5.

[60] James Hannam, *God's Philosophers*, p. 336

9. The Purging Fires

[61] Augustine, *Faith, Hope and Charity*, chapters 68–69.

[62] See C. S. Lewis, *Letters to Malcolm, Chiefly on Prayer* (Geoffrey Bles, 1964), chapter 20.

[63] Purgatory didn't only divide Catholics and Protestants; it was also a stumbling block to reunion between the Eastern Orthodox Church and the Catholics at the Council of Ferrara-Florence (1538–9). The Eastern Orthodox, represented by Mark of Ephesus, didn't believe in a literal purging fire, the 'treasury of merits' or paying for indulgences. This doesn't mean, though, that the Eastern Orthodox churches hold

the Protestant view. Eastern Christians still believe in the possibility of further purification after death and offer prayers for the dead in the belief that this will help them.

64 This schism is sometimes known as the Western Schism to distinguish it from the events of 1054.

65 Papal infallibility is the idea that the pope is preserved from making error in binding decisions on faith and morals for the whole church; it doesn't mean that everything that the pope says or does is believed to be without error.

66 According to the *Catechism of the Catholic Church* (see sections 1373–1375), transubstantiation is the idea that Christ becomes present in the Lord's Supper by the conversion of the bread and wine into his body and blood. The word 'transubstantiation' itself reflects the substance theory of the Greek philosopher Aristotle, who distinguished between the underlying reality (or *substance* – in this case, the body, blood, soul and divinity of Christ) of a thing and its ongoing external appearance (or *accident* – in this case, bread and wine).

67 In the West, at that time, people only received the bread in communion due to concerns about spilling the blood of Christ, though this has since changed. In the East, the usual practice is for the congregants to receive the bread together with the wine, using a spoon.

10. Reform and Radicalism

[68] The words Martin Luther is reputed to have said in his defence at the Diet of Worms, 1521.

[69] Peter Kreeft, *Fundamentals of the Faith* (Ignatius Press, 1990), chapter 44.

[70] Baptismal regeneration is the belief that a person is 'born again' by God through baptism.

11. Fighting over Faith

[71] Although this chapter looks at conflict between Christians, it is good to bear in mind that this period also saw the city of Constantinople fall to Turkish armies in 1453 (and be renamed Istanbul), with Turkish armies advancing into Europe and reaching as far as Vienna. Thus the fighting over faith also includes a long period of warfare between Christian and Muslim armies.

[72] See John Calvin, *Institutes of the Christian Religion*, 3.23.7.

[73] The most famous of these is Michael Servetus, who denied the Trinity and the baptism of babies (as well as calling for Calvin's arrest and execution) and who was burned at the stake in Geneva in 1553. Calvin himself seems to have wanted Servetus to be beheaded rather than burned to death.

[74] The term 'Reformed' originally described those

churches which came out of the Reformation, but soon started to be used in a more limited sense to describe those churches which followed the Calvinist stream. While the word 'Reformed' is often used today as the opposite of Arminian, it is worth remembering that Arminius himself was a minister of the Dutch Reformed Church until his death and regarded himself as also being Reformed.

[75] There is some doubt as to whether John Calvin himself believed in limited atonement.

[76] The Geneva Bible (1560) was the first translation in English to use verse numbers (which had been invented in 1551). Later editions of this ground-breaking translation included maps and commentary on passages, making it, in effect, the first study Bible in English. Some of these comments were critical of the idea of the divine right of kings, a view which James I held strongly; this might, in part at least, explain his eagerness to replace the Geneva Bible with a version commissioned by himself.

12. Wake Up Britain!

[77] This cost included opposition from parts of the established church and 'polite society', as well as more direct confrontation with hostile elements in the crowd who would often pelt the preachers with stones and other objects – even dead cats!

[78] This idea was not original to John Wesley but was probably developed from his contact with the Moravians. These were part of a wider movement among German-speaking Christians in the 17th and 18th centuries called Pietism, which reacted against the formality of the official state churches. Pietists would often hold household meetings to pray, worship and study Scripture together.

13. Doubts and Revolutions

[79] See C. S. Lewis, *Mere Christianity*, book 2, chapter 11, for more on this idea.

[80] Stanley J. Grenz and Roger E. Olsen, *20th-Century Theology: God and the World in a Transitional Age* (IVP, 1992), p. 17.

[81] See chapter eight for more detailed discussion as to why this isn't true.

14. Wars and Rumours of Wars

[82] Other Nazi victims included some Christian opponents of Nazism, such as Dietrich Bonhoeffer.

[83] There have also been movements which could be described as being part of the religious left, such as Christian Socialism.

[84] See the section on spiritual gifts in chapter two for a historical perspective on how these gifts operated in the early centuries of the church.

[85] Bruce Shelley, *Church History in Plain Language* (fourth edition Thomas Nelson, 2013), p. 457.

15. Where Now?

[86] G. K. Chesterton, *The Napoleon of Notting Hill* (Bodley Head, 1904).

ROOTED
RECONNECTING WITH THE HISTORY OF THE CHURCH
EDWARD RHODES